MASTERING THE CALIFORNIA DMV EXAM

What You Need to Pass the DMV Permit Test in 2024 - 2025

ROAD SCHOLAR PUBLISHING

MASTERING THE
CALIFORNIA DMV EXAM

Legal Notice:

Disclaimer Notice:

Table of Contents

Introduction

Getting your California driver's license is more than just passing a written exam and a driving test. It's a gateway to freedom, independence, and opportunity. Imagine the possibilities! With a license, you can:

- **Run errands:** Now, there's no more relying on parents, friends, or buses for grocery shopping, picking up prescriptions, or grabbing takeout.
- **Explore California:** Hit the beach in San Diego, hike Yosemite, or visit the vibrant cities—all on your own schedule.
- **Have a social life on your terms:** Meet friends for movies, attend concerts, or explore new restaurants, all without depending on others for rides.

A driver's license also opens doors in the job market. Many employers, especially outside major cities with robust public transportation, consider a license a necessity. It shows you're reliable, responsible, and able to get yourself to work locations that might not be easily accessible by bus or train. Not to mention the fact that driving itself can be a job!

Learning to drive teaches valuable skills that go beyond operating a vehicle. You'll develop skills such as:

- **Decision-making:** You'll constantly assess road conditions, anticipate other drivers, and make quick decisions.

- **Focus and concentration:** Staying alert and attentive behind the wheel translates to better focus in other areas of life.
- **Time management:** Planning routes and factoring in traffic helps you become more time-conscious.

Getting your license signifies a step towards adulthood. You'll be responsible for maintaining your car (or using it responsibly if you don't own one), following traffic laws, and prioritizing safety.

With a license, you can be there for friends and family. You can offer rides to errands, appointments, or social gatherings, especially for those who may not have their own licenses or access to reliable transportation.

Do understand that a driver's license is not a right, but a privilege that you need to work for. Earning it signifies you understand the responsibility that comes with operating a motor vehicle safely and following the rules of the road. The knowledge in this book will not only help you pass the DMV test, but also ensure you're a prepared, confident, and safe driver on California's roads.

California DMV Process

Getting your California driver's license might seem daunting, but it can be a smooth ride if you know what to expect. Let's break down the process so that you know what to expect.

Step 1: Permit Test

The permit test assesses your knowledge of California traffic laws, road signs, and safe driving practices. Here's what to expect:

- **Preparation:** Review the information contained in this book, and practice with the mock exam at the end of the book until you get all the questions right!
- **The test:** The computer-based test has multiple-choice questions in 35 languages, including English. You'll need to score at least 80% to pass.
- **Retesting:** Worry not if you don't pass the first time (though, if you follow the steps in the book, you're highly likely to pull that off). You can retake the test twice online, but if you fail both attempts, you'll need to visit a DMV office for a third try.

Step 2: Driving Test

This part of the test will gauge your ability to observe safety measures while operating a vehicle. Here's how to prepare:

- **Practice:** Get behind the wheel with a licensed driver (25 or older if you're under 18) and practice maneuvers like parallel parking, three-point turns, and navigating different road types. We will go over how to do these things in this book as well.
- **The test:** A DMV examiner will ride with you and assess your skills in handling the vehicle, following traffic laws, and making safe decisions.

Step 3: License Issuance

Once you pass the driving test, congratulations! You'll receive a temporary license valid for 90 days while your permanent license is processed. Your official license will arrive by mail within a few weeks.

The DMV process is designed to ensure you have the knowledge and skills to be a safe driver. By preparing diligently and approaching the tests with confidence, you'll be cruising down the road with your California driver's license in no time!

So, are you ready to start learning everything you need to know to pass the test? Great, see you in Chapter 1!

Chapter 1

How to Use This Book

Before we get into the nitty-gritty of what you need to know to pass the test, you'll need to know how to use this book effectively. This will help you to pass the first time and get the most out of this book!

Navigating the Handbook

This handbook is your key to unlocking the road. But, with so much information packed within its covers, navigating it effectively becomes crucial for passing the DMV test.

The handbook is divided into distinct sections, each playing a different role. Sections like Road Signs and Markings walk you through understanding the varied signs and road markings on California's roads, while the Mock Exam gives you a chance to practice the test. However, the heart of your studies lies in sections like Laws and Regulations and Safe Driving Tips. These sections equip you with the knowledge and skills to navigate California's roads safely and responsibly—knowledge that forms the core of the written test.

Don't underestimate the power of visuals! The handbook is filled with diagrams and charts that illustrate traffic signs, road markings, and proper vehicle positioning. At the end of the book, there is a full-length practice exam, which you can try taking before and after reading through the chapters. That way, you can keep track of how your mastery improves over time. Don't just passively read through them; actively engage by answering them and reviewing the explanations provided.

Dedicate specific times each week to studying the handbook. Break down the sections into manageable chunks and create a schedule that allocates time for each. Focus on mastering one section before moving on to the next. This focused approach prevents information overload and ensures that you retain what you learn.

Treat the test like a driving scenario, but bear in mind that some information is more important than others. While understanding vehicle registration procedures might be helpful, they likely won't feature heavily on the test. Pay more attention to road rules, traffic signs, and safe driving practices. The handbook itself will offer clues about what's important.

Passive reading won't get you far. Employ active reading strategies to maximize information retention. As you read, underline key points, jot down questions in the margins, and summarize what you've learned in your own words.

This handbook is more than just a test prep tool. By navigating it strategically and employing these techniques, you'll transform the handbook from a hurdle into a road map to your California driving permit.

Overview of the Book

This book is designed to not just help you pass the California DMV test, but also transform you into a safe and confident driver.

The book closely follows the structure and content of the California Driver's Handbook. Each chapter corresponds to a specific section of the official handbook, ensuring you cover all the topics tested on the DMV exam. You'll find in-depth explanations of traffic laws, right-of-way rules, and safe driving practices, all presented in a clear and concise manner.

The book begins with an introduction to the licensing process, followed by dedicated chapters tackling crucial topics like:

- **Traffic signs and signals:** Understanding different types of signs, their meanings, and proper responses
- **Right-of-way rules:** Determining who has the right-of-way in various contexts (such as intersections and merging lanes)
- **Safe driving practices:** Covers everything from maintaining proper following distances to handling emergencies and adverse weather conditions
- **California Vehicle Code:** Getting familiar with the Code's sections that govern driving behavior

Each chapter dives deep into the relevant information, highlighting key points through bold text, summaries, and visual aids. Complex concepts are broken down into simpler explanations, ensuring clarity and comprehension.

The book goes beyond simply preparing you for the test by emphasizing the importance of developing lifelong driving habits. This includes topics like:

- **Distracted driving:** Understanding the dangers of texting, talking on the phone, and other distractions behind the wheel
- **Sharing the road:** Learning how to safely interact with pedestrians, cyclists, and motorcycles
- **Defensive driving techniques:** Developing strategies to anticipate and avoid potential hazards on the road

Don't just skim through the practice questions. Treat them as you would the actual exams Time yourself, analyze your mistakes, and refer back to the corresponding chapters in the book for clarification. Don't just pick answers; think through the scenarios and explain your reasoning. This process will help you deepen your understanding and hone your critical thinking skills, which are crucial for safe driving.

In the next chapter, we will start by going through traffic laws and regulations. See you there!

Chapter 2

Traffic Laws and Regulations

You're well on your way to earning your California driver's license. Before hitting the road, you'll have to master the rules that govern safe and legal driving. Let's examine California's traffic laws and regulations. We'll explore everything from right-of-way at intersections and proper turning techniques to handling traffic signals and understanding road signs. By mastering these essential elements, you'll not only be prepared for your DMV exam but also gain the foundation for becoming a responsible and courteous driver.

Right-of-Way Rules at Intersections, Stop Signs, and Yield Signs

Intersections can be tricky, but understanding right-of-way rules keeps everyone safe.

Intersections Without Traffic Control Devices

Yield to the right when approaching an uncontrolled intersection (no stop signs, yield signs, or traffic signals). The vehicle on your **right** has the right-of-way, regardless of who arrived first. If no vehicles are to your right, proceed with caution after checking for oncoming traffic from both directions.

At uncontrolled intersections, making left turns requires extra caution. You must **yield the right-of-way** to all oncoming traffic, including vehicles going straight and turning right, as well as those already in the intersection.

Intersections With Traffic Signals

These can be broken down in several types:

- **Protected left turns:** These turns have a dedicated green arrow allowing you to turn left without oncoming traffic. However, always double-check for turning vehicles and pedestrians before proceeding.
- **Unprotected left turns:** These turns are made during a green light for your direction, but you must yield to oncoming traffic turning left, going straight, or already in the intersection.
- **Right turns:** On a green light, you may turn right after yielding to pedestrians in the crosswalk.
- **Red lights:** Always come to a complete stop and remain stopped until the light turns green.
- **Yellow lights:** A yellow light warns of an impending red light. Slow down safely but avoid stopping abruptly to avoid rear-end collisions.

Right-of-Way for Pedestrians and Cyclists

Pedestrians in marked crosswalks always have the right-of-way, even when there's no signal. Yield to cyclists who are treating a marked bike lane as an extension of the sidewalk or following traffic signals as vehicles.

Stop Signs

Slow down gradually as you approach a stop sign. Be prepared to make a complete stop. A complete stop means all vehicle movement ceases, not just a rolling stop.

In the scenario of a complete stop, the right-of-way belongs to the vehicle that arrived at the stop sign first. If multiple vehicles arrive at the same time, the vehicle to the right proceeds first. (Refer back to the "yield to the right" rule).

All-way stop signs require vehicles on all approaches to come to a complete stop. Two-way stop signs only require vehicles on the road with the stop signs to stop; those on the through road have the right-of-way.

Yield Signs

Slow down and be prepared to stop if necessary. Yield the right-of-way to all oncoming traffic already in the intersection, pedestrians in crosswalks, and turning vehicles.

Take note that, unlike with stop signs, you don't need to come to a complete stop at a yield sign *if* the way is clear. But, if there's oncoming traffic, pedestrians, or cyclists, you need to yield the right-of-way.

A yield sign might not apply on a multi-lane highway with an on-ramp. In those cases, traffic merging onto the highway must yield to vehicles already in the lane.

Always be aware of your surroundings and anticipate the actions of other drivers, pedestrians, and cyclists.

Speed Limits and Adjusting for Conditions

Speed is one of the most important factors in safe driving. The faster you drive, the more devastating a crash could be. However, driving too slowly can also cause an accident.

Types of Speed Limits

There are three types of speed limits:

- **Posted speed limits:** These are the legal maximum speeds displayed by numerical signs along the road. They are set based on factors like road design, traffic volume, and surrounding development. Exceeding the posted speed limit is a traffic violation.
- **Advisory speed limits:** These are recommendations displayed on signs with a lower speed than the posted limit. They are used in areas with specific hazards or changing conditions, like sharp curves or merging zones. While not legally enforceable, it's wise to follow advisory speed limits for your safety.
- **Speed limits by vehicle type:** Some roads might have different speed limits for different vehicle types. Trucks, buses, and motorcycles might have lower speed limits than cars due to their size and maneuverability. Pay close attention to signs indicating these variations.

Adjusting Speed for Conditions

Safe driving isn't just about following posted speed limits. You also need to adapt your speed to real-time conditions. Specifically, you need to take the following into consideration:

- **Weather:** Rain, snow, fog, and high winds all reduce visibility and road traction. Slow down significantly in these conditions to maintain control of your vehicle.
- **Road conditions:** Uneven pavement, potholes, gravel, or construction zones require reduced speeds for a smoother and safer ride.
- **Traffic volume:** Heavy traffic congestion necessitates slower speeds to allow for frequent stopping and maneuvering.
- **Visibility:** During nighttime or in low-light conditions, slow down to allow for more reaction time in case of hazards.

Techniques for Adjusting Speed

Regularly scan the road ahead to anticipate potential hazards and adjust your speed accordingly.

The two-second rule is a simple yet effective technique. Choose a fixed object on the road ahead (like a sign) and ensure at least two seconds elapse between you passing that point and the vehicle in front of you passing it. Increase the following distance in poor conditions or with larger vehicles.

When slowing down, ease off the gas pedal to allow the engine to slow the car down gradually, reducing reliance solely on the brakes. Avoid erratic speed changes, and maintain a speed and distance that allows you to react safely to changing situations.

Lane Changing, Passing, and Merging Techniques

Navigating multiple lanes requires smooth and safe maneuvers.

Lane Changing

Always activate your turn signal well in advance (at least 100 feet) before initiating a lane change to alert other drivers of your intention.

Before and during your lane change, use your mirrors and perform a blind spot check by turning your head to look over your shoulder, in order to ensure that there are no vehicles in your blind spot.

Don't change lanes

- when approaching intersections, curves, or on-ramps.
- if there's not enough space in the lane you're trying to enter.
- when another vehicle is already signaling a lane change into your lane.

Once you confirm it's safe, accelerate smoothly to match the speed of traffic in the lane you're entering before completing the lane change.

Passing

The general rule for passing is to **go around another vehicle on the left side.**

Make sure the coast is clear before you even think about moving into the left lane. There shouldn't be any vehicles approaching from the opposite direction that could cause a head-on collision.

Let the driver you're passing know what you're planning to do by turning on your left turn signal well in advance. This gives them a chance to adjust their speed if necessary. Once you've confirmed it's safe, check your left mirror and blind spot to make sure there are no vehicles next to you. Then, smoothly change lanes into the left lane.

Keep a good distance between your car and the vehicle you're passing. Don't hug their bumper. Aim for enough space so you can comfortably maneuver back into the right lane when you're done passing.

Once you're alongside the slower vehicle, accelerate smoothly to get past them. Do not stay in their blind spot longer than you have to. After you've passed the vehicle, use your right turn signal and check your right mirror and blind spot again before merging back into the right lane. Make sure there's enough space for you to get back in safely without cutting off another driver.

Here are other things you need to consider when passing:

- **Never pass on the right shoulder.** This is illegal and very dangerous.
- **Don't pass in oncoming traffic lanes.** Only pass in designated left lanes.

- **Don't pass in zones with restricted passing.** Look out for signs or pavement markings indicating no passing zones, like on curves or near intersections.
- **Yield to oncoming traffic.** If you start to pass and see oncoming traffic that hinders your passage before reaching your lane, slow down and abandon the pass.

Merging

When merging onto a freeway or highway from an on-ramp, yield the right-of-way to vehicles already in the traffic lane. Increase your speed to match the flow of traffic in the lane you're merging into before entering the lane. Don't come to a complete stop on the ramp, as this can disrupt traffic flow.

Maintain a safe following distance from the vehicle in front of you in the lane you've merged into. This enables you to react promptly in case of sudden braking.

Understanding Traffic Signals

Traffic signals are the conductors of our roadways, keeping traffic flowing smoothly and safely. Let's briefly recap what these signals stand for.

- **Red light:** A red light means **STOP**. Come to a complete stop before the crosswalk line and remain stopped until the light turns green.
- **Yellow light:** A yellow light warns of an impending red light. Slow down safely but avoid stopping abruptly to prevent rear-

end collisions. If you can safely stop before entering the intersection when the light turns yellow, do so. Otherwise, proceed with caution through the intersection.

- **Green light:** A green light allows you to proceed through the intersection with caution. However, always yield to pedestrians in crosswalks and oncoming vehicles turning left that have already entered the intersection.

- **Left turn signals:** Some intersections have dedicated left turn signal phases. These may be:

  o *Protected left turn:* A green arrow specifically for left turns allows you to make a left turn without oncoming traffic. However, always double-check for turning vehicles and pedestrians before proceeding.

  o *Unprotected left turn:* A green light for your direction allows left turns, but you must yield to oncoming traffic turning left, going straight, or already in the intersection.

- **Flashing yellow light:** A flashing yellow light treats the intersection as a yield sign. Proceed with caution, drive slowly, and let all vehicles and pedestrians already in the intersection have the right-of-way.

- **Red turn arrow:** A red turn arrow prohibits turning in that direction. Wait for a green turn arrow or green light (depending on the intersection) before turning.

- **Pedestrian crossing signals:** These signals with walking figures or flashing red lights indicate designated crosswalks for pedestrians. Yield the right-of-way to pedestrians in crosswalks, even when there's no signal.

- **Special signals:** Some intersections might have additional features like school zone signals that flash yellow during designated times or countdown timers indicating how long each light phase will last. Always follow the specific instructions provided by these signals.

Malfunctioning Traffic Signals

In rare cases, a traffic signal might malfunction.

Look for signs like unlit signals, conflicting light patterns, or damaged signal fixtures. Proceed with caution as if it's a four-way stop intersection. Come to a complete stop, make eye contact with other drivers, and yield the right-of-way to vehicles that arrived before you or those to your right.

Following Distances and Safe Driving Intervals

Leaving enough space between your vehicle and the one in front is crucial for safe driving.

Following Distance

A safe following distance is the critical space between your vehicle and the one in front that allows you enough time to react safely if they brake suddenly. It prevents rear-end collisions and gives you more control on the road.

One thing to keep in mind here is the **three-second rule**. Choose a fixed object on the road ahead (like a sign) as the vehicle in front of you passes it. Count "one-thousand-one, one-thousand-two, one-thousand-three" after they pass the point. If you pass the same point before finishing your count, you're following too closely.

Increase the following distance as your speed increases. For example, at highway speeds, consider a four-second or even greater following distance. In bad weather (rain, snow, fog), slick roads, or heavy traffic, significantly increase your following distance to allow for more reaction time.

Instead of counting seconds, you can also choose a fixed object on the road ahead and ensure at least one car length appears between your vehicle and the one in front as they pass that point. Increase the car lengths as your speed or the need for caution increases.

Safe Driving Intervals

Maintaining a safe space cushion around your vehicle allows room for unexpected maneuvers by yourself or other drivers. This buffer zone can prevent accidents caused by sudden lane changes, merging vehicles, or debris on the road. The size of your safe driving interval depends on several factors:

- **Speed:** Higher speeds require a larger safe interval to allow for increased stopping distances.
- **Traffic conditions:** Heavy traffic necessitates a larger cushion to react to sudden braking or lane changes.
- **Driver reaction time:** Factor in your own reaction time, which can vary based on age, alertness, and distractions.

An important aspect of safe driving is anticipating potential hazards. By leaving room for escape maneuvers, you can avoid collisions caused by breakdowns, drunk drivers, or sudden stops.

Highways, Freeways, and Rural Roads

Not all roads are created equally, and you'll need to know the differences among them.

Highways and Freeways

Highways and freeways are high-speed, controlled-access roads designed for efficient long-distance travel. These roads have designated entrance and exit ramps to prevent stopping or merging from local roads. Highways and freeways typically have multiple lanes in each direction, allowing for faster traffic flow. Posted speed limits on these roads are generally higher than on local roads. Specific rules apply on highways and freeways:

- Maintain your lane and avoid weaving between lanes unless absolutely necessary.
- Use turn signals well in advance before changing lanes. Proceed to the shoulder only during emergency situations.
- Never stop on the shoulder unless your vehicle is disabled.
- Some highways might have minimum speed requirements. Be aware of these posted limits and avoid impeding the flow of traffic by driving too slowly.

Rural Roads

Rural roads offer scenic views, but they also present unique challenges. Rural roads are often narrower, with blind curves, limited shoulders, and potential for wildlife crossings. Be aware of farm equipment and slow-moving vehicles that might share the road.

Passing on rural roads requires extra caution due to limited visibility. Only attempt to pass when there's sufficient oncoming lane space and clear sightlines in both directions. Oncoming traffic might not always be readily visible due to curves or hills. Reduce your speed and be prepared to yield the right-of-way if necessary.

Posted speed limits on rural roads are typically lower than on highways. Always adjust your speed to accommodate these lower limits and be prepared for unexpected hazards. Also, weather conditions can significantly impact driving on rural roads. Reduce your speed significantly in rain, fog, or snow.

In the next chapter, we will explore how to share the road safely with other drivers, cyclists, and pedestrians.

Chapter 3

Sharing the Road Safely

California's roads are a bustling network shared by cars, trucks, motorcycles, bicycles, and pedestrians. Navigating this diverse environment requires more than just knowing the rules of the road. It demands a spirit of cooperation and awareness. So, let's explore how to interact safely with other drivers, cyclists, and pedestrians to ensure a smooth and accident-free roadway for everyone.

Sharing the Road With Others

Acing your California DMV written test requires understanding how to navigate the roads safely, whether you're on foot, bike, or motorcycle.

Pedestrians

As a pedestrian, you need to understand that your safety hinges on respecting traffic signals and crosswalks. Always wait for the green light or WALK signal before crossing, and utilize designated crosswalks whenever available. They provide a safe zone for you to navigate intersections.

Sidewalks are your primary walking space. If no sidewalk exists, walk on the left shoulder of the road, facing oncoming traffic, to maximize visibility. Stay alert and avoid distractions like phones or music that can impede your awareness of your surroundings.

During nighttime hours, when visibility is reduced, make yourself more noticeable by wearing reflective clothing. This simple step can significantly increase your chances of being seen by drivers.

From a Driver's Point of View

As a driver, you must be extra vigilant when approaching intersections and crosswalks. When you see pedestrians crossing with a green light or WALK signal, make sure to always yield the right-of-way. Crosswalks are designated for pedestrian safety, so be prepared to stop and allow them to cross completely. Pedestrians have the right to use sidewalks. Be mindful of pedestrians on the sidewalk, especially when turning corners or entering/exiting parking lots. Avoid blocking sidewalks with your vehicle.

Pedestrians can be engrossed in their phones or music players, which make them less aware of their surroundings. Always be on the lookout for potentially distracted pedestrians, especially near crosswalks and intersections. Slow down and be prepared to stop if you have to.

During nighttime or low-light conditions, pedestrian visibility decreases significantly. Look out for reflective clothing worn by pedestrians and be extra cautious in areas with limited street lighting.

Bicycles

Cyclists in California have the same rights and responsibilities as motorists on the road. This means obeying traffic signals, stopping at stop signs and red lights, and yielding the right of way when necessary.

Ride with the traffic flow, instead of going against it. Designated bike lanes offer a dedicated space for cyclists, but if these are unavailable, use the rightmost lane, positioning yourself predictably. Signal your intentions clearly using proper hand signals before turning or stopping. Don't assume that drivers will anticipate your movements.

California law mandates helmet use for anyone under 18, but it's wise for all cyclists to wear a properly fitted helmet that meets safety standards. Consider additional safety gear like reflective clothing and bright lights, especially during low-light conditions.

From a Driver's Point of View

Cyclists have the same rights and responsibilities as motorists. This means they are expected to obey traffic signals, react accordingly to stop signs, and yield the right of way when necessary. As a driver, be prepared to share the lane with cyclists and anticipate their movements.

Cyclists often navigate tight spaces. Be aware of designated bike lanes and avoid impeding their flow. If there are no bike lanes, watch for cyclists positioned in the rightmost lane and give them ample space when passing. Pay attention to their hand signals for turning or stopping.

Cyclists are more vulnerable than drivers in the event of an accident. Maintain a safe following distance behind cyclists and avoid making sudden lane changes that could cut them off. Similar to pedestrians, cyclists are less visible during low-light conditions. Look out for reflective clothing and bright lights used by cyclists, and be extra cautious when sharing the road at night, dusk, ordawn.

Motorcycles

Hitting the road on a motorcycle requires a Class C license with a motorcycle endorsement. This endorsement signifies that you've passed a written test and a skills test specific to motorcycles.

Motorcycles are smaller and less visible than cars, so lane positioning is crucial. Avoid lingering in blind spots; instead, strategically position yourself in the lane to be clearly seen by surrounding traffic.

Due to shorter braking distances compared to cars, maintaining a safe following distance behind other vehicles is even more important on a motorcycle. California's following distance law applies to motorcycles as well.

Never underestimate the importance of headlights. Unlike some states, California mandates motorcycles to have their headlights on at all times, day or night. This ensures you are visible to other drivers on the road.

From a Driver's Point of View

Motorcycles are significantly smaller than cars and can easily disappear into blind spots. Always check your mirrors thoroughly before changing lanes and be aware of the wider turning radius required by motorcycles. Avoid lingering alongside motorcycles in your lane.

Motorcycles have shorter braking distances compared to cars. Maintaining a safe following distance behind motorcycles is essential to allow them ample room to stop safely. California's following distance law applies to motorcycles as well.

Unlike some states, California mandates motorcycles to have their headlights on at all times. However, don't solely rely on the motorcycle's headlight for visibility. Actively scan the road for motorcycles, especially during low-light conditions or on roads with limited visibility.

School Zone Safety

California takes student safety extremely seriously, and a significant portion of the DMV written test focuses on proper behavior in school zones.

As you approach a school zone, your vigilance should immediately heighten. These areas are designated with specific signage to warn drivers of the presence of children, and these signs are not suggestions. As a matter of fact, they're legal mandates.

Be on the lookout for flashing yellow lights, which are a precursor to a school bus stopping or children crossing the street. These yellow lights serve as a warning to slow down and prepare for a complete stop.

Reduced speed limit signs are also prevalent in school zones. These signs indicate a lower speed limit than the standard speed limit, typically around 25 mph. The posted speed limit is the absolute maximum, and you may need to adjust your speed even further based on weather conditions, traffic congestion, or the presence of pedestrians.

School Buses

School buses are the primary mode of transportation for many children, and their bright yellow color is a clear indicator that extra caution is required. However, the most crucial signal to watch for is the flashing red lights on the top front and back of the bus.

These flashing red lights, coupled with the extended stop sign arm, signify that the bus has come to a complete stop to pick up or drop off children. When you see this combination, bear in mind that California law mandates a complete stop from **both directions** of traffic, regardless of the presence of a median separating the lanes.

This complete stop applies until the red lights are deactivated and the stop sign arm is retracted. Only then can you proceed with caution, ensuring all children are clear of the roadway before moving forward.

Even when a school bus is not actively loading or unloading children, maintaining a safe following distance is essential. School buses are larger and heavier than most vehicles, and they require more distance to come to a complete stop. Following too closely puts you at risk of rear-ending the bus if it makes a sudden stop for a child crossing the street.

The temptation to pass a stopped school bus, especially when there seems to be no immediate danger, can be strong. However, succumbing to this urge is not only illegal but also incredibly dangerous. Children tend to be unpredictable and may dart out from behind the bus without warning.

Passing a stopped school bus with flashing red lights is a guaranteed way to fail your DMV test, and more importantly, it puts the lives of innocent children at risk.

Understanding Traffic Control Devices

California's roads are a complex network, and sometimes, unexpected situations like construction or accidents necessitate temporary changes in traffic flow. The California DMV written test places significant emphasis on your ability to understand and navigate these changes using traffic control devices. Here's a breakdown of what you need to know to conquer the test and become a safe driver on the road.

Cones, Barrels, and Channelization Devices

Common temporary traffic control devices include cones, barrels, drums, and channelization devices like barriers or delineators. While their shapes may vary slightly, their vibrant orange color serves as a universal warning. As such, proceed with caution!

Not all cones are the same. While the standard orange signifies a general hazard area, some situations require a more specific warning. Be aware of these color variations:

- **White cones:** These usually mark traffic lanes or pedestrian walkways within a construction zone. White cones serve to separate these lanes and walkways from the active work area.

- **Blue cones:** Often used for parking restrictions or utility work zones, blue cones indicate areas where stopping or parking is prohibited.

Flags

Flags are another communication tool employed in construction zones. These brightly colored flags, usually red or orange, are used by flaggers to direct traffic flow. Pay close attention to the flagger's hand signals, which follow a standardized system, and adjust your speed and lane position accordingly.

Detour Signs

When you encounter a construction zone, detour signs become your trusted companions. These diamond-shaped signs with an orange background provide essential information about alternate routes to bypass the construction area. Look for clear instructions on the detour sign, including the direction of the detour and the estimated distance. Following these directions will help you navigate the maze and reach your destination safely.

Lane Closure Markings

Temporary lane closures are often indicated by painted markings on the road surface. Solid white lines separate traffic lanes, while double solid white lines indicate a no-passing zone. Dashed white lines, on the other hand, may be used to create buffer zones between traffic lanes and the construction area. Be mindful of these lane markings and adjust your position accordingly.

Yielding to Emergency Vehicles

Acing your California DMV written test requires a strong understanding of how to react when encountering emergency vehicles. These flashing lights and sirens signal a critical situation, and yielding the right of way is not just courteous. It's the law.

Lights and Sirens

Emergency vehicles on a mission are unmistakable. Whether it's the red and blue lights of a police car, the piercing siren of an ambulance, or the steady red lights of a fire truck, these combined visual and auditory cues scream urgency. The California DMV emphasizes your ability to recognize these emergency vehicles promptly.

Don't rely solely on what's directly in front of you. Utilize your mirrors and peripheral vision to scan for approaching emergency vehicles from behind or on intersecting roads. Early detection allows you ample time to react appropriately.

Once you identify an approaching emergency vehicle with its lights and sirens activated, California law mandates that you yield the right-of-way immediately. This means moving your vehicle to a safe location and coming to a complete stop.

Ideally, pull over to the right shoulder of the road as far away from traffic as possible. If you're on a multi-lane road, move to the rightmost lane and stop. Never stop in the middle of the road or an intersection, as this can obstruct the emergency vehicle's path and create a further hazard.

While yielding, turn on your hazard lights (also known as emergency flashers) as an additional safety measure. This blinking light pattern further communicates your intention to stop and increases your vehicle's visibility, especially during low-light conditions.

The urge to continue driving after an emergency vehicle pass can be strong. However, California law emphasizes the importance of waiting until the emergency vehicle, along with any accompanying vehicles, passes a safe distance before proceeding.

A safe distance is generally considered to be when you can no longer see the emergency vehicle in your rearview mirror. This ensures the emergency vehicle has ample space to maneuver and complete its critical mission without the risk of being impeded by traffic flow that restarts too quickly.

Navigating Large Trucks and Buses

California's diverse roadways are shared by vehicles of all shapes and sizes. But large trucks and buses pose unique challenges for car drivers. Acing your California DMV written test requires a firm grasp of how to navigate these behemoths safely.

The Blind Spots of Large Vehicles

Think of a large truck or bus as a giant rectangle on wheels. Unfortunately, the driver's view from the cabin doesn't encompass the entire rectangle. These extensive blind spots, particularly on the sides and directly behind the vehicle, are danger zones for smaller cars. The California DMV emphasizes your ability to recognize these blind spots.

Never linger in a large vehicle's blind spot. This means avoiding driving directly next to a truck or bus for extended periods. Use your mirrors to gauge your position relative to the larger vehicle and adjust your lane position accordingly. If you can't see the truck driver in their mirror, they likely can't see you either.

Keeping a Safe Distance

Following distance is important for safe driving, but it becomes even more critical when sharing the road with large trucks and buses. Their immense weight translates to significantly longer stopping distances compared to your car. If you maintain a larger following distance behind these vehicles, you'll have enough time to react in case of a sudden stop.

California's following distance law applies to all vehicles, but adhering to a safe distance behind large trucks and buses goes beyond legal obligation. It's a proactive safety measure. Be mindful of potential hazards that might cause a large vehicle to stop abruptly, such as road debris or a slower vehicle ahead. Increasing your following distance provides a buffer zone to react safely to these situations.

Passing

Passing a large truck or bus can be tempting, especially on long stretches of road. However, the California DMV emphasizes the importance of safe passing maneuvers. Never attempt to pass unless there's ample space and clear visibility in the oncoming lane. Look out for oncoming traffic and potential hazards like blind curves or no-passing zones before initiating a pass.

Once you've confirmed it's safe to pass, complete the maneuver swiftly and decisively. Don't linger alongside the large vehicle after passing. Merge back into the right lane promptly to minimize the time you spend in the oncoming lane and avoid creating a dangerous situation for yourself and others.

In the next chapter, we will go over the various road signs and markings. We'll find out how to identify them and what they mean.

Chapter 4

Road Signs and Markings

A cing the section on road signs and markings is all about understanding the visual language of the road. This chapter will equip you with the knowledge to confidently navigate any sign or marking thrown your way, ensuring a smooth ride toward your driver's license. Buckle up and get ready to become a sign-savvy driver!

Understanding Road Signs

Mastering these visual cues is crucial for passing the California DMV written test and becoming a confident driver. Let's look at the three main types of signs you'll encounter: regulatory, warning, and informational.

Regulatory Signs

Easily recognizable by their circular shape and red, white, or black backgrounds with clear white symbols, regulatory signs establish mandatory actions or restrictions. These are the law enforcers, and disobeying them can lead to tickets, fines, or (even worse) accidents. Stop signs, yield signs, and speed limit signs, No Turn on Red signs all fall under this category. Remember, these signs are non-negotiable. When you see a stop sign, you come to a complete halt, not a rolling stop. Speed limits are the maximum safe speeds, not suggestions for how fast you can push your car. Heeding these signs is not just about avoiding fines; it's about demonstrating respect for the rules of the road and ensuring everyone's safety.

The most common regulatory signs are:

Stop sign (Octagonal shape, red with white lettering): A complete stop is required before proceeding.

Yield sign (Inverted triangle shape, yellow or red with black lettering): Drivers must slow down and yield the right-of-way to oncoming traffic or pedestrians.

Speed limit sign (Rectangular shape, white with black lettering): This indicates the maximum speed limit in miles per hour (mph) that drivers may travel on a particular road.

Do Not Enter sign (Rectangle with red background and white lettering): This prohibits drivers from entering a particular road or highway.

One Way sign (Rectangle with white background, black arrow, and black lettering): This indicates that traffic may only proceed in one direction.

Parking signs (Various shapes and sizes, with combinations of red, white, black, and green): These regulate parking restrictions. Examples include time limits, no parking zones, and permit-only parking.

Turn prohibition signs (Circular shape, red with white symbol or lettering): These prohibit drivers from making a specific turn (left, right, or U-turn) at that location.

Lane control signs (Rectangular shape, white with black symbols or lettering): These indicate restrictions on lane usage, such as turn lanes, carpool lanes, or high-occupancy vehicle (HOV) lanes.

 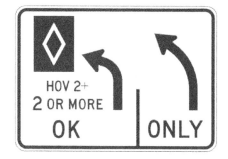

Pedestrian crossing signs (Rectangular shape, white with black symbols or lettering): These warn drivers of a crosswalk and the presence of pedestrians.

School zone signs (Usually diamond-shaped with orange or yellow background and black lettering): These alert drivers that they are entering a school zone, which means that they might need to slow down or stop to give way to children on the move.

Warning Signs

These bright yellow diamond-shaped signs, emblazoned with black symbols, serve as friendly warnings of potential hazards ahead. A sharp curve might be lurking around the next bend, merging traffic could create congestion, or deer might be crossing in a designated zone. These signs are not there to scare you but to prompt you to adjust your speed and driving behavior accordingly. Seeing a winding road sign? Slow down and take the turn with caution. Spot a merging traffic sign? Be prepared to adjust your lane position and maintain a safe following distance. By heeding these warnings, you can anticipate potential dangers, navigate them smoothly, avoid accidents, and keep yourself and others safe.

The most common warning signs are:

Animals: Deer Crossing, Wild Pigs in Area, Watch for Horses

Road Features: Curve Ahead, Winding Road, Narrow Bridge, Divided Highway Ends, Merging Traffic, Lane Ends

Traffic Control: Stop Ahead, Yield Ahead, Traffic Signal Ahead, Do Not Pass, One Lane Road, Two-Way Traffic Ahead

Hazards: Slippery When Wet, Loose Gravel, Falling Rock, Low Shoulder, Dip, Crosswind

Other Warnings: Fog Ahead, Dust Storm, High Winds, Work Zone, Children Playing

Informational Signs

Unlike their regulatory and warning counterparts, informational signs don't dictate your actions or warn of immediate danger. Instead, they act as helpful guides. These rectangular signs, typically blue or green with white lettering or symbols, provide valuable information for navigation. They'll tell you where to find the nearest rest area, alert you of upcoming exits, or even guide you towards specific destinations. While not carrying the legal weight of regulatory signs, informational signs can be lifesavers, especially when you're unfamiliar with the area. Spotting a blue sign with a gas station symbol? You know it's time to fill up. Seeing a green sign with an arrow pointing towards a scenic viewpoint? A quick pit stop for a breathtaking view might be in order.

Here are the most common informational signs by color:

Green Signs

These signs offer directional guidance, indicating exits, upcoming cities, or distances to destinations.

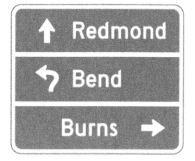

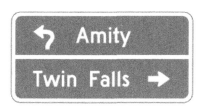

Brown Signs

These rectangular signs point out recreational areas like state parks, campgrounds, or points of interest.

Blue Signs

These signs provide information on motorist services like gas stations, rest areas, restaurants, and hospitals.

Road Markings

Understanding these markings is not just about aesthetics; it's essential for safe driving and acing the California DMV written test.

Lane Lines

These lines separate traffic lanes, ensuring organized flow and preventing collisions. You will come across two main types of lane lines: solid and dashed.

Solid lines, typically painted in white or yellow, are the unyielding boundaries separating opposing traffic. Think of them as a clear message: "Do Not Cross!" These lines are in place for your safety and the safety of others. Crossing a solid line, except in designated turn lanes with proper signaling, is a recipe for disaster.

Dashed lines, on the other hand, represent a more flexible separation between lanes. They indicate that lane changes are permitted, but with a crucial caveat: caution. Before making a lane change with a dashed line, always check your mirrors and blind spots, signal your intention clearly, and ensure it's safe to proceed. Remember that, even with dashed lines, courtesy and defensive driving are paramount.

Crosswalks

Think of crosswalks as designated zones where pedestrians have the right-of-way to safely cross the street. These areas are typically marked by a combination of painted lines and signage. You might see parallel solid white lines forming a striped pattern, often nicknamed "zebra stripes," or pedestrian crossing signs with a walking figure symbol. Spotting any of these markings should trigger an immediate response: Yield to pedestrians!

Whether a pedestrian is already in the crosswalk or simply approaching it, you need to come to a full stop so that they can cross safely.

Stop Lines

Stop lines are the thick white lines painted across your lane before an intersection or a stop sign. They mark the exact spot where your vehicle must come to a complete stop.

Coming to a complete stop before reaching the stop line is crucial. Not only is it the law, but it also allows you to assess the intersection for oncoming traffic, pedestrians, and potential hazards before proceeding. Stopping past the stop line not only violates traffic laws but also creates a dangerous situation by blocking the crosswalk and hindering pedestrian movement.

Lane Designation Markings

These are arrows or symbols painted directly on the pavement, often in conjunction with traffic signals. They act as visual reinforcements, specifying which lanes have the right-of-way during specific signal phases.

For example, you might see a left turn arrow painted on the ground next to a traffic signal. This is the signal's backup singer, emphasizing that only vehicles in that lane are permitted to turn left when the green arrow illuminates. Similarly, you might see straight lane arrows paired with a green light, indicating that only those lanes can proceed straight through the intersection. By understanding these painted cues, you'll avoid confusion and ensure you're following the right-of-way designated by the traffic signal and its pavement markings.

Turn Lane Markings

These lanes are clearly marked with painted left or right turn arrows on the pavement. Using these designated turn lanes is not just a courtesy; it's a crucial safety measure tested on the California DMV written test.

Designated turn lanes ensure smooth traffic flow and prevent vehicles from cutting each other off. By using the appropriate turn lane and aligning your vehicle with the painted arrow, you communicate your turning intention clearly to other drivers, creating a more predictable and safe environment.

Pedestrian Signals

Traffic signals aren't just for vehicles; they cater to pedestrians as well. This is where pedestrian signals come in. These can be countdown timers or illuminated walking person symbols displayed on the traffic signal itself. They act as a countdown to safety for pedestrians, indicating when it's safe for them to cross the street.

The California DMV emphasizes pedestrian safety, and understanding these signals is key to passing the written test. When you see the pedestrian signal illuminate a walking figure or initiate a countdown, it's time to yield the right-of-way to any pedestrians waiting to cross.

Navigating Special Zones

While standard road signs provide the general rules of the road, specific areas require extra caution.

School Zones

You will know when you are in a school zone as they will be clearly marked with prominent orange diamond-shaped signs displaying a black school symbol. You may also encounter flashing yellow lights near the signs, further emphasizing the presence of a school.

School zones typically have reduced speed limits compared to regular roadways. This is because children, often unpredictable and smaller in stature, are more vulnerable in traffic collisions. By adhering to the posted speed limits in school zones, you're contributing to a safer environment for these young pedestrians. Remember, the California DMV emphasizes responsible driving around schools, so mastering these signs is key to passing the written test.

But the presence of a school zone goes beyond reduced speed limits. It also demands increased awareness. Be extra vigilant for children who might be walking, cycling, or waiting for the bus near the school. Always anticipate the unexpected and be prepared to slow down or stop suddenly if a child darts into the street.

When you see a school bus with its flashing red lights activated and the stop sign extended, it's a clear instruction: Come to a complete stop, regardless of the direction you're traveling from. This law is strictly enforced to ensure the safety of children entering and exiting the bus.

Construction Zones

These areas, marked by prominent orange diamond-shaped signs with black symbols depicting construction work ahead, demand a different approach to driving. While the familiar yellow diamond signs warn of general hazards, these orange signs signal a specific hazard: ongoing construction work.

The most crucial aspect of navigating construction zones is adhering to the posted speed limits. These limits are often lower than usual to accommodate workers and machinery present on the road. By reducing your speed, you make the surrounding area safer for everyone concerned.

You will also need to obey flaggers. These individuals, often wearing bright vests and wielding hand-held stop signs, are the temporary traffic directors. When a flagger signals you to stop, slow down, or merge, it's a mandatory instruction.

Be prepared for potential lane closures, sudden merging situations, and uneven road surfaces. Always anticipate the unexpected and adjust your driving accordingly to navigate these temporary obstacles safely.

Hazardous Materials Zones

These materials, ranging from flammable liquids to explosives, require extra caution while transporting. These zones are marked by prominent orange diamond-shaped signs with black symbols depicting the specific hazard: a flame for flammable materials, an explosion symbol for explosives, and so on.

Understanding the specific hazard being transported is vital. Flammable materials require a safe distance to minimize the risk of fire in case of an accident. Explosives demand even greater caution, with wider following distances and strict adherence to any additional instructions displayed on the signs.

The most important principle in hazardous materials zones is maintaining a safe distance from the vehicles transporting these materials. Though the specific distance might be indicated on the signs themselves, always prioritize creating ample space between your vehicle and the hazardous cargo. This ensures minimal risk in case of an accident or unforeseen situations.

In the next chapter, we will explore the process of pre-drive checks and the role they play in keeping you safe.

Chapter 5

Pre-Drive Checks

The pre-drive check is important not just for passing the test, but for keeping you safe on the road! This chapter will transform you from a nervous test-taker into a confident driver by demystifying the pre-drive checklist. We'll break down each item, explain its importance, and guide you through demonstrating your knowledge to the examiner.

The Importance of Routine Vehicle Maintenance

Acing the California DMV written test requires understanding the importance of routine vehicle maintenance. This goes beyond keeping your car looking shiny, though. It's more about ensuring your car's safety, reliability, longevity, fuel efficiency, and even its resale value.

What if you're cruising down the highway when your brakes suddenly grind or a tire blows? These scenarios highlight the critical role of maintenance in preventing accidents. Have regularly scheduled checkups and service identify potential problems before they escalate, in order to ensure optimal performance of essential safety features like brakes, tires, and steering components. A well-maintained car translates into a safer driving experience for you, your passengers, and everyone on the road.

Let's face it: Getting stranded on the side of the road is never convenient. Routine maintenance acts as a shield against such situations. By proactively addressing minor issues like low fluid levels or worn-out parts, you significantly reduce the risk of unexpected breakdowns. This preventive approach keeps your car reliable and ensures you reach your destination without unnecessary delays or stress.

Think of your car as a complex machine. Just like any machine, its parts experience wear and tear over time. Regular maintenance helps minimize this wear and tear by keeping components lubricated, clean, and functioning properly. This not only extends the overall lifespan of your vehicle but also saves you money in the long run. You'll avoid costly repairs that might arise from neglecting maintenance and letting minor issues snowball into major problems that require complete part replacements.

Fuel costs can put a dent in your wallet. By keeping your car well-maintained, you can save some money on gas. Worn-out spark plugs, dirty air filters, and improper tire pressure can all contribute to decreased fuel efficiency. By following the recommended maintenance schedule, you ensure that your car operates at its peak performance, maximizing the number of miles you get out of every gallon of fuel.

When it comes time to sell your car, a documented history of routine maintenance becomes a valuable selling point. Potential buyers are more likely to be interested in a vehicle that has been consistently cared for. A car that has been properly maintained has a higher resale value than a neglected vehicle. Regular maintenance demonstrates to buyers that you've taken pride in ownership and that the car is in good condition.

The Pre-drive Check

Taking a few minutes before setting off can allow you to identify potential problems early on, thus preventing accidents and costly repairs down the road. So, let's look at the different parts of the checklist and how to do them.

Tire Check

Your tires are the only things contacting the road; they are responsible for grip, handling, and a smooth ride. Regularly checking their condition is necessary for safety and performance.

Pay close attention to how full your tires look. Underinflated tires will appear sunken on the sides, while overinflated ones will bulge outwards. Proper inflation is vital for safe handling and fuel efficiency.

Uneven tread wear is a red flag. Look for areas where the tread seems shallower than others. This could indicate alignment problems or improper inflation. Here's a handy trick: Insert a penny upside down between the tread grooves. If you see the top of Lincoln's head, your tread depth might be getting low and it might be time to consider replacing your tires. Refer to your owner's manual for the minimum recommended tread depth.

Inspect your tires closely for any cuts, bulges, or cracks on the sidewall or tread. These can be potential safety hazards and might lead to blowouts. If you notice any such damage, don't hesitate to get your tires checked by a professional immediately.

Don't rely solely on your eyes. Grab a good quality tire pressure gauge. It's a simple and affordable tool that can make a big difference.

Your car's recommended tire pressure, measured in pounds per square inch (PSI), is crucial information. Look for a sticker on the driver's door jamb or consult your owner's manual. This value might vary depending on whether your car is carrying a load or not.

Unscrew the valve stem cap (the little cap on the tip of the tire valve) and press the gauge firmly onto the valve stem. You'll hear a hissing sound briefly, then a reading will appear on the gauge. Compare this to the recommended PSI and inflate the tire using an air pump at a gas station or an air compressor if needed. Remember, never adjust the pressure when the tires are hot after driving.

Light Check

Your car's lights keep you safe and aid in clear communication with other drivers, especially at night.

Start by turning on your car's ignition and setting it to "accessory" mode (if your car has it) or by starting the engine. This will power up all the lights without requiring the car to be in drive. Systematically activate each set of lights: headlights (low and high beams), taillights, brake lights, turn signals (both left and right), and hazard lights.

Get out of your car and walk around the entire vehicle. This allows you to visually confirm that each light is functioning properly and emitting a bright, clear beam. Pay close attention to the turn signals:

They should blink rhythmically and not flicker or stay lit continuously.

Have someone stand behind your car while you press on the brakes. They should confirm that the brake lights illuminate brightly when you press down on the pedal. Engage the reverse gear and check if the dedicated white reverse lights come on at the back.

Headlight misalignment can be a safety hazard for you and oncoming traffic. While a basic check involves observing the beam pattern on a wall in a dark environment, it's recommended to visit a mechanic or tire service center periodically to ensure proper alignment.

If you notice that a particular light appears dimmer than usual, it might be a sign that the bulb is nearing the end of its lifespan. Don't wait for a complete burnout; replace it as soon as possible. Replacing burnt-out bulbs is a relatively simple task for most cars. Refer to your owner's manual for specific instructions on how to access and replace the bulbs in your vehicle. If you're not comfortable doing it yourself, many service stations or mechanics can replace them for you quickly and easily.

Fluid Check

Keeping your car running smoothly relies on a delicate balance of several vital fluids. Pop the hood open and identify the engine oil dipstick. It's usually a brightly colored loop or handle protruding from the engine block. Consult your owner's manual if you have difficulty finding it. Pull out the dipstick entirely, wipe it clean with a rag, and reinsert it fully back into its place. Then, pull it out again to observe the oil level. The dipstick will have markings indicating the minimum and maximum safe oil levels.

While checking the level, pay attention to the oil's condition. Healthy oil should be a clear amber color. If it appears dark brown, black, or gritty, there is a need for an oil change.

If the oil level is low, consult your owner's manual for recommendations on topping up or scheduling an oil change based on your car's mileage and oil type.

Find the windshield washer fluid reservoir under the hood. It's typically a translucent plastic container with a filler cap, often labeled with washer fluid symbols. Open the cap and check the fluid level. If it's low, top it up with the appropriate washer fluid type recommended in your owner's manual. Avoid using household cleaning products or water alone, as they can damage the washer fluid system or freeze in cold weather.

Engine coolant plays a critical role in regulating your car's engine temperature. The reservoir that holds the coolant can be located in various places depending on your car's make and model. Refer to your owner's manual for its exact location and identification.

Once you've located the coolant reservoir, check the fluid level. It should typically fall between the minimum and maximum fill lines indicated on the reservoir. Healthy coolant should also be a bright green, orange, or yellow color. A brownish or rusty color might indicate coolant degradation or contamination, requiring a coolant flush and refill.

Mirror Check

Your car's mirrors are like extra eyes on the road, expanding your field of vision and eliminating hidden dangers.

The primary function of your rearview mirror is to provide a clear and unobstructed view of traffic following you. Adjust the tilt of the mirror using the lever located at its base. Ideally, you should see a majority of the car behind you, with minimal focus on your own vehicle's interior.

Unlike the rearview mirror, your side mirrors should offer a view that minimizes the image of your own car and maximizes the view of the lanes beside you. While seated in your normal driving position, adjust the side mirrors outwards until you can just barely see the edge of your car along with the lane beside you. This way, you'll eliminate blind spots and be able to detect vehicles approaching from behind or alongside you without having to crane your neck.

Getting used to proper mirror positioning might take some practice. Remember, a quick glance at the mirrors should be a natural part of your routine whenever you change lanes or check for traffic behind you. Don't rely solely on mirrors—a shoulder check (turning your head briefly to look over your shoulder) is still an important safety practice to confirm what you see in the mirrors.

Brake Check

Your brakes play a key role in ensuring the safety of everyone riding inside your vehicle. With the car in motion at a slow speed (ideally in a safe, controlled environment), gently apply the brakes. Pay close attention to any unusual noises. Healthy brakes should operate quietly. If you hear grinding noises when applying the brakes, it's a red flag. This sound often indicates worn-out brake pads or rotors, and it necessitates a visit to a mechanic as soon as possible.

A firm and responsive brake pedal is what you're aiming for. When you press down on the pedal, it should provide a reassuring sense of resistance and stop the car confidently without requiring excessive pressure.

A spongy or soft feeling when pressing the brake pedal can indicate air in the brake lines or other issues. This can significantly reduce braking efficiency, and as such, you'll need to consult a professional mechanic right away.

While not a substitute for a professional check-up, you can also perform a quick visual inspection of your brakes. Look for any obvious signs of wear and tear on the brake pads or rotors through the gaps in your wheels. Your owner's manual might have specific recommendations for brake checks or service intervals based on your car's make and model. Refer to it for additional guidance.

How to Do the Pre-drive Check During the test

The California DMV pre-drive check focuses on two main aspects: ensuring your vehicle meets minimum safety standards and testing your knowledge of the car's operation. So, let's look at how to apply what we've discussed in this chapter when we take the test.

Vehicle Safety Check

The DMV examiner will ask you to locate and demonstrate your knowledge of the following items related to your vehicle's safety:

- **Driver's window:** Verify that the driver's side window can be fully opened and closed.
- **Windshield:** You and the examiner must have a clear and unobstructed view through the windshield. No cracks that can impede visibility are allowed.
- **Mirrors (Two required):** Your vehicle must have at least two mirrors. There should be one outside mirror on the driver's side. The second mirror can be either outside on the passenger side or inside the vehicle on the center console. Both mirrors must be securely fastened and unbroken, and they should provide a clear view for the driver.
- **Turn signals:** The examiner will ask you to activate both the left and right turn signals (front and back) to confirm they are functioning properly.
- **Brake lights:** Similar to turn signals, you'll be asked to engage the brakes while the examiner observes the functionality of both rear brake lights.
- **Tires:** Each tire must have a minimum tread depth of 1/32 inch in at least two adjacent grooves, meeting the legal requirement for safe driving. The examiner will likely check for any bald spots or signs of damage like bulges or cuts that could lead to a blowout.

Driver's Knowledge of Vehicle Operation

Here are some of the things the examiner might ask you to demonstrate during the pre-drive check.

- **Parking brake:** Locate and demonstrate how to set and release the parking brake. The examiner will confirm its functionality to ensure it holds the vehicle securely when engaged.
- **Horn:** The horn must be designed for your specific vehicle and be in proper working order. The sound produced by your vehicle's horn should be audible from a minimum distance of 200 feet. No novelty horns like bicycle horns are allowed.

Blind Spots

Blind spots are zones around the rear pillars of your car that remain hidden from your view even when using the mirrors. These areas can easily conceal motorcycles, bicycles, or other vehicles, thus posing a significant safety risk when changing lanes or merging with traffic.

Ensure you can see your entire back window through the rearview mirror without needing excessive head movement. This allows for a quick and comprehensive view of traffic behind you.

Adjust the side mirrors outwards until you can just barely see the edge of your car along with the lane beside you in the mirror. Resist the urge to angle them inwards to see more of your car.

With this proper adjustment, a swift glance in the side mirror should reveal any vehicles approaching from behind or alongside you in the lane beside your car. The mirror will capture the approaching vehicle as it exits your blind spot and enters your peripheral vision, thus allowing you to make safe lane changes and maneuvers.

Seat Belt Use

Seat belts are the single most effective defense against injury or death in a car accident. They work by distributing the tremendous forces of a crash across a wider area of your body, minimizing the risk of serious injuries. They also significantly reduce the chance of being ejected from the vehicle in a collision, which is often fatal.

When it comes to the shoulder belt, it should be positioned comfortably across the center of your chest. It should never rest on your neck, as this can cause serious injuries in a crash. Imagine the shoulder belt supporting your chest bone, not your collarbone. Ensure the shoulder belt is not resting on your arm. This can be uncomfortable and restrict your ability to maneuver the steering wheel safely.

The lap belt should fit low and tightly across your hips, below your abdomen. A high lap belt resting on your stomach can cause serious internal injuries in a crash. Double-check that there are no twists in the belt. A twisted belt can reduce its effectiveness in a collision.

Ensure the seat belt buckle is securely fastened and the latch is engaged properly. A loose belt won't provide optimal protection.

Taking a few seconds to adjust your seat belt properly can make a world of difference in the event of a crash.

Alright! You are all set to ace the pre-drive check. In the next chapter, we will go through driving maneuvers and techniques.

Chapter 6

Driving Maneuvers and Techniques

You've learned the rules of the road, and now it's time to translate that knowledge into smooth, safe driving. Let's break down essential maneuvers like starting, stopping, turning, and changing lanes, and let's ensure that you can handle them with precision and control. You'll also learn defensive driving techniques that keep you safe in unexpected situations.

Mastering Steering Techniques

Your steering wheel is the primary tool for controlling your car's direction.

Imagine the steering wheel as a clock. The ideal hand positions are either at 10 and 2 o'clock, or at 9 and 3 o'clock. These positions offer optimal leverage for smooth turning and quick reaction times. Think of your hands as cradling a large ball, thumbs resting lightly on the inside rim of the wheel. This firm but relaxed grip provides the necessary control without tensing your arms, which can lead to jerky movements.

Avoid jerky or sudden movements that can throw you off course and unsettle the vehicle. Instead, focus on making gradual and controlled inputs with both hands. Imagine tracing a smooth curve with your hands, mirroring the desired path of the car.

Don't just react to what's directly in front of you. Constantly scan the road ahead, identifying upcoming turns, curves, and lane changes. This allows you to initiate smooth, progressive steering inputs before you actually reach the turn, ensuring a comfortable and controlled path through the maneuver.

Not all turns are created equal. Tight corners require more significant steering input than gentle curves. As such, you have to adjust your movements based on the situation you'll encounter. For minor corrections to your lane position, use small, controlled movements of the wheel. As turns become sharper, gradually increase the amount of steering input you provide. This ensures you maintain a centered position in your lane while avoiding the dreaded oversteering.

Oversteering occurs when you turn the wheel too sharply, causing the car to lose grip and potentially skid. Imagine turning the wheel too much like trying to steer a shopping cart with a broken wheel—it becomes unstable and unpredictable. To avoid this, practice maintaining a centered position in your lane. When making turns, focus on smooth, controlled adjustments. If you feel the car start to lose grip, ease off the steering wheel slightly.

Countersteering

While the focus of your driving test will be on safe, controlled maneuvers, there's a valuable technique worth knowing for emergency situations, and that is countersteering. This advanced skill can help you regain control if your car skids, a situation where your tires lose traction with the road surface. Countersteering is not essential for passing the DMV test, and attempting it without proper training can be dangerous. However, with supervised practice, it could save your vehicle and your life.

Imagine driving on a slick road or taking a sharp corner a little too fast. Suddenly, you feel a loss of control. Your car might start to skid, its direction dictated by the momentum of the slide rather than your steering input. This is because your tires have lost traction with the road, rendering your normal steering efforts ineffective.

So, what do you do when your car is in a skid? You'll need to turn the steering wheel in the direction of the skid. If your car skids to the right, your initial instinct might be to crank the wheel left, in the direction you want to go. However, in a skid, this will likely worsen the situation. Instead, by turning the wheel right (which is the same direction of the skid), you're essentially telling the car to "follow the skid" momentarily. This allows the tires to regain some grip, and as they do, you can then initiate the correction.

Once you've felt a slight improvement in traction, it's time for the correction. With a smooth, controlled movement, turn the steering wheel back in the opposite direction (left in our example) to straighten out your car's path. This correction should be proportional to the severity of the initial skid. A small skid might require a minor counter-turn, while a larger skid might necessitate a more significant correction. The key is to be gentle and avoid overcorrecting, which can send you into a skid in the opposite direction.

Countersteering is a complex maneuver that requires precise timing, good coordination, and a cool head in a stressful situation. Attempting this technique on public roads without proper training can be dangerous. If you're interested in learning countersteering, seek out a qualified driving instructor who can guide you through the process in a safe, controlled environment. Through practice in a controlled setting, you can develop the muscle memory and reflexes needed to react effectively in an emergency skid situation.

Backing Up

Backing up a car might seem like a simple task, but it's a maneuver that demands your full attention and proper technique. A minor mistake can lead to a collision, so let's delve into the steps that ensure a safe and controlled reverse.

Before even thinking about putting the car in reverse, a thorough check of your surroundings is essential. Start by using your mirrors to scan for pedestrians, vehicles, and any obstacles behind your car. Don't forget those blind spots! A quick glance over each shoulder eliminates any unseen dangers lurking in these zones. Once you're confident the coast is clear, activate your hazard lights. This not only alerts others of your intention to back up but also serves as a warning to slow down and be cautious around your vehicle.

Backing up should be a deliberate and controlled maneuver. Shift into reverse, gently press down on the accelerator, and ease back slowly. Remember, you have limited visibility behind you, so take your time and allow yourself ample reaction time to any unexpected hazards. Avoid jerky movements or quick changes in direction, as these can throw you off course and make it difficult to maintain control of the vehicle.

While your mirrors are your primary tools for monitoring your surroundings during a backup, they can't capture everything. Take a quick glance over your shoulder as well. This glance helps confirm what you see in the mirrors and gives you a more complete picture of what's behind the car. Don't rely solely on one method: A multi-sensory approach is key for safe backing up. As you continue to reverse, make it a habit to constantly check your mirrors and blind spots, keeping your head on a swivel and staying aware of your surroundings.

Once you've reached your desired stopping point and confirmed it's safe to come to a complete stop, don't forget to straighten your wheels before shifting into park. Leaving your wheels turned while parked can put unnecessary strain on the steering components, potentially leading to future problems. A quick turn of the wheel in the opposite direction of your reverse ensures your car is parked straight and avoids any potential damage.

Parallel Parking

Parallel parking can be daunting, as it's a test of skill and spatial awareness. But fear not! By following these steps and referencing the accompanying diagrams, you'll be parallel parking like a pro in no time!

The first step is to identify a suitable parking space. Ideally, you want a spot that's roughly 1.5 times the length of your vehicle. This extra space provides some breathing room for maneuvering. Once you've found your target, activate your turn signal to indicate your intention to park, then slow down to a safe speed.

Pull up alongside the car parked in front of the space you've chosen. Aim to maintain a distance of about two feet between your car and the parked car. Adjust your position until you can see just the edge of the parked car in each mirror. This ensures you're parallel and at a safe distance.

Double-check your mirrors and blind spots to ensure it's safe to proceed. Then, with confidence, turn the steering wheel fully in the direction opposite the curb (right turn if you're parallel parking on the right side of the road). This will position your car to begin swinging into the parking space.

Shift into reverse, gently press on the accelerator, and start backing up slowly. Continuously check your mirrors and glance over your shoulder to monitor the space behind you. Your goal is to align your rear bumper with the back corner of the car in front. Once you've reached this point, come to a complete stop.

Straighten your steering wheel completely and then begin backing up slowly again, but this time at an angle. Use your mirrors to judge the distance between your car and the curb. You want to be close enough to the curb without scraping your wheels, but not so close that you can't fit your car in.

Once your car is at a 45-degree angle and getting close to the curb, it's time for the final turn. Sharply turn the steering wheel in the direction of the curb (left turn for parallel parking on the right side of the road). This will straighten out the front wheels of your car and allow you to smoothly fit into the parking space.

Continue backing up slowly and make small corrections to your steering wheel as needed until your car is fully parked within the space. Ideally, your car should be centered in the space, with a straight line between your front and rear wheels. Avoid being too close to the curb or the car in front. If you need to make minor adjustments after coming to a complete stop, you can carefully pull forward or reverse a bit to achieve the perfect park.

Hill Starts and Preventing Rollback

The first line of defense against a rollback on a hill is the parking brake, also known as the emergency brake. This simple tool acts as a safety net, preventing your car from inching backward while you transition from the brake pedal to the accelerator. The key here is to engage the parking brake **before** coming to a complete stop on the incline. This way, you can take your foot off the brake pedal to control the accelerator without the car unexpectedly rolling back.

Many newer vehicles come equipped with a technological guardian angel called Hill Start Assist (HSA). This nifty feature essentially acts as a temporary electronic parking brake. When activated (usually by default on hills), HSA automatically holds the brakes for a few seconds after you release the brake pedal, giving you precious time to find the clutch's bite point and apply gas without rolling back. If your car boasts this feature, take some time to understand how it works and familiarize yourself with any activation or deactivation buttons.

Whether you're relying on the traditional parking brake or the helping hand of HSA, the core of a successful hill start lies in coordinating your pedals.

Gently lift your foot off the brake pedal while slowly pressing down on the clutch pedal. Feel for the "bite point," that sweet spot where the clutch starts to engage and the engine revs begin to rise. This is where the engine starts providing enough power to overcome the hill's incline.

Once you've found the bite point, maintain steady pressure on the clutch pedal and **gradually** increase pressure on the accelerator. As the engine revs pick up, you can slowly release the parking brake (or HSA will automatically disengage) while continuing to ease off the clutch. This coordinated effort should propel your car smoothly uphill without a hint of rollback.

You now know how to use your steering wheel like a pro. In the next chapter, we will look at safe driving practices and habits.

Chapter 7

Safe Driving Practices and Habits

I n this chapter, we will be exploring safe driving practices and habits that will not only help you ace your DMV test but, more importantly, keep you and others safe on the road for years to come.

We'll explore defensive driving techniques, essential road awareness skills, and the importance of maintaining a hazard-free driving mindset. By understanding these key principles, you'll transform from a nervous permit holder into a confident, competent driver prepared to navigate California's diverse roadways.

Why Defensive Driving and Hazard Anticipation Are Your Best Friends

Sure, following the rules of the road is important. But defensive driving is more than just that. It's a philosophy, a way of approaching the road with a keen eye for potential trouble and a proactive plan to steer clear of it. It's about anticipating what might go wrong before it does and taking steps to minimize the risk.

Defensive drivers aren't just passive observers. They're constantly scanning their surroundings, like detectives piecing together a scene. They notice the car that seems a little too close in the next lane, the brake lights that appear further ahead than usual, and the weather that might make the road slick. They understand that other drivers, even the careful ones, can make mistakes. By anticipating these possibilities, defensive drivers are ready to react calmly and effectively.

The benefits of this approach are clear. Fewer accidents means fewer people getting hurt, yourself included. It also gives you more confidence behind the wheel. You're no longer a passenger in a chaotic dance of traffic, but someone in control, navigating the road with a sense of awareness and preparation. There's even a chance that your defensive habits could lead to lower insurance premiums, a reward for being a responsible driver.

The key lies in constant vigilance. Your eyes become scanners, not just fixed on the car in front but sweeping the entire scene. Is that driver in the next lane weaving erratically? Are rain clouds gathering on the horizon? Is there a pothole lurking just beyond the crest of a hill? By actively searching for potential dangers, you give yourself a chance to react before they become a real threat.

Will that impatient driver try a risky lane change? Might that child on the sidewalk dart into the street? By considering these possibilities, you can position your vehicle and adjust your speed to create a buffer zone, a safe space cushion that absorbs the unexpected. The following distance between you and the car in front should be large enough to react comfortably to a sudden stop. Similarly, leave ample room on all sides of your vehicle, giving yourself room to maneuver if needed. By anticipating the potential for mistakes from yourself and others, as well as creating a margin for error, you transform the unpredictable nature of the road into a space where you're prepared for anything.

Why Distractions Are Your Worst Enemy

These can be anything from fiddling with the radio to grabbing a quick bite. The most dangerous culprit is often the one clutched in our hands: the cell phone. The problem with distractions is that they chip away at the three pillars of safe driving: visual awareness, manual control, and cognitive focus. Glancing down to text takes your eyes off the road, leaving you blind to potential hazards. Balancing a burger in one hand makes it harder to react quickly if you need to steer. And engaging in a conversation, even hands-free, diverts your mental focus from the critical task of navigating the road.

Cell phones are particularly insidious because they combine all three distractions. Talking, texting, or using navigation apps steals your visual attention with the bright screen, reduces your manual control as you hold or tap the phone, and saps your cognitive focus as you process the conversation or information on the screen. It's like trying to drive a car while simultaneously juggling blindfolded, with one hand tied behind your back as you recite complex math equations in your head.

The consequences of this divided mind are dire. Studies have shown that distracted driving is just as dangerous, if not more so, than driving under the influence of alcohol. Reaction times slow, spatial awareness diminishes, and the ability to make sound judgments evaporates. In the blink of an eye, a minor distraction can morph into a major accident.

Cell phones are not the only culprits of distraction when you're on the road. The truth is, anything that diverts your attention from the road can be dangerous. Grabbing a rogue french fry that tumbled from the passenger seat, fumbling with the radio to silence a blaring commercial, or even the allure of a perfectly winged eyeliner application—these seemingly harmless actions can all have life-or-death consequences.

The danger lies in the way these distractions disrupt the delicate balance required for safe driving. Eating forces you to take your eyes off the road and juggle utensils while steering. Fiddling with the stereo diverts your focus from the traffic symphony around you. While passengers can be great companions, their need for your immediate attention—whether it's a question, a heated debate about the latest movie, or a sudden need for you to mediate a sibling squabble—can pull your focus away from the critical task at hand.

So how do we combat these distractions, both the technological and the social? The first step is a commitment to putting your phone away entirely. Silence notifications, stow it in the glove compartment, or employ a phone-blocking app—anything to remove the temptation of a quick glance or text reply. Remember, a missed call or message is a small price to pay for your safety and the safety of others on the road.

When it comes to other distractions, cultivate a sense of mindfulness. Plan your meals before you get behind the wheel. Adjust the climate control or radio settings before you start driving. And politely yet firmly explain to passengers that their safety, and yours, depends on you focusing on the road. Pull over to a safe location if a conversation absolutely cannot wait.

Why DUI/DWI Is a Recipe for Disaster

Getting behind the wheel is a privilege, a responsibility to operate a complex machine at high speeds while surrounded by others. But introduce alcohol or drugs into the equation, and this delicate balance crumbles. These substances act like a fog descending on the mind, impairing the very faculties crucial for safe driving.

The effects are far-reaching. Judgment, the compass that guides our decisions on the road, becomes clouded. Reaction times slow to a sluggish crawl, leaving you lagging behind the split-second demands of traffic. Coordination, the intricate dance between your mind and body, falters. Steering becomes imprecise, braking distances stretch into an eternity, and the delicate act of navigating a lane transforms into a perilous tightrope walk. Even vision, the window to the world around you, can be distorted, blurring crucial details and compromising your ability to see potential hazards.

The danger doesn't stop at a single drink or a small dose. Even seemingly insignificant amounts of alcohol or drugs can be enough to tip the scales, pushing a driver from capable to catastrophic. It's a gamble with terrifying odds, a game where the potential losses are measured in shattered lives and irreversible heartbreak.

The legal consequences of DUI/DWI further underscore the severity of this offense. It's not just a traffic violation; it's a crime with real repercussions. A DUI conviction can lead to a suspended license, making it impossible to get to work, school, or appointments. Steep fines can drain your finances. Jail time can leave you separated from loved ones and disrupt your entire life.

The potential consequences, both personal and legal, are far too high. If you're under the influence, the only responsible option is to find a safe ride home. There's no shame in admitting you're impaired, but there's immeasurable tragedy in ignoring the warning signs and getting behind the wheel. Choose safety, choose responsibility, and choose to keep yourself and others safe on the road.

Thankfully, there are responsible alternatives that ensure everyone arrives safely. Before the festivities even begin, designate a driver who will remain sober throughout the night. This trusted friend becomes your hero, your chariot guide back to reality, ensuring a safe and worry-free journey home.

Technology can also be your knight in shining armor. Ride-sharing services like Uber or Lyft offer a convenient and readily available option. With a few taps on your phone, a sober driver arrives at your doorstep, whisking you away from temptation and towards your destination. Public transportation, though it might require a bit more planning, is another excellent choice. Trains, buses, or even subways offer a safe and affordable way to navigate the city after a night out.

if you've been drinking or using drugs, getting behind the wheel is never an option. It's a decision that not only puts your own life at risk, but also jeopardizes the safety of everyone on the road. This responsibility doesn't just fall on the driver's shoulders. Never get into a car with someone who is visibly intoxicated. Speak up, encourage them to find a safe way home, and offer to call a ride-sharing service or a taxi. In these situations, even a seemingly harmless car ride can turn deadly.

Road Rage

Traffic. It's a universal experience, a slow-moving beast that can test even the most patient driver. Add to this the inconsiderate drivers, unexpected delays, and the simmering stress of daily life, and a recipe for road rage can easily boil over. But, before you allow frustration to morph into aggressive driving, understand that you're not powerless against this inner monster.

Road rage is the ugly stepchild of anger, fueled by a potent cocktail of impatience, entitlement, and a perceived lack of control. Traffic congestion becomes a personal attack, slow drivers transform into villains, and every minor inconvenience feels like a deliberate act of malice. Aggressive driving behaviors like tailgating, weaving through lanes, speeding, and hurling insults only escalate the situation, putting yourself and others at risk.

The key to managing road rage lies in recognizing the warning signs. Are you starting to tighten your grip on the steering wheel? Is your heart pounding a frantic rhythm against your ribs? Do you find yourself clenching your jaw and muttering curses under your breath? These are all red flags that anger is brewing. Take a deep breath, a conscious effort to break the escalating cycle. Acknowledge your frustration, but don't let it control you.

Instead, take a more defensive approach. Focus on keeping a safe following distance, let go of the need to be 'first,' and be an example of smooth, predictable driving. Imagine yourself in a bubble of calmness, unfazed by the chaos around you.

Other drivers are human too. They might be lost, late for an appointment, or simply having a bad day. Instead of assuming malice, offer a silent word of understanding. Challenge yourself to find humor in the absurdity of the situation. Put on some calming music, or use this time to practice mindfulness techniques like deep breathing or progressive muscle relaxation.

Deep breathing is a simple yet powerful tool. Inhale slowly and deeply through your nose, feeling your belly expand. Hold for a count of four, then exhale slowly through your mouth. Repeat this cycle a few times, and feel the tension drain away with each exhale.

Beyond your own emotions, focus on what you can control: your own driving. Maintain a safe following distance, giving yourself ample space to react to unexpected situations. Avoid weaving through lanes or speeding to "get ahead." Instead, concentrate on smooth, predictable movements. Imagine yourself in a protective bubble, unfazed by the potential storms brewing around you.

Leave a healthy buffer zone between your car and others. This extra space provides a physical and psychological cushion, reducing the feeling of being pressured or needing to react abruptly to their movements.

If you encounter a truly aggressive driver, do not engage. Getting into a shouting match or responding with similar aggression only escalates the situation and puts everyone at risk. If possible, pull over to a safe location, away from the aggressive driver. Once you're calm and clearheaded, call the police and report the incident.

Staying calm behind the wheel isn't just about managing your own emotions; it's about creating a safe space for yourself and those around you.

Night Driving

Nighttime presents a unique set of challenges for drivers. Reduced visibility becomes the ever-present foe, demanding a shift in strategy and heightened awareness. Safe nighttime navigation lies in acknowledging the limitations imposed by darkness. Headlights pierce the gloom, but their reach is finite. Oncoming traffic becomes a symphony of glowing orbs, often blurring the details of the road ahead. Pedestrians and cyclists, who used to be easily spotted, can vanish into shadowy figures. This is not the time for bravado or autopilot driving. A cautious and measured approach is the only way to navigate the night safely.

Headlights are your lifeline to the road. Don't wait until you're enveloped in complete darkness to turn them on. Dusk is the time to flick them on, a signal to yourself and others that you're aware of the changing light conditions. High beams can be helpful on deserted stretches of road, but remember, courtesy is key. The moment you see oncoming headlights or a vehicle in your rearview mirror, dim those high beams. There's nothing more disorienting than a sudden blast of light in the dead of night.

During the day, familiar landmarks and road markings guide your perception of distance and speed. At night, these visual cues can be muted or disappear altogether. Reducing your speed is an essential compromise. Allow yourself ample reaction time in case of unforeseen hazards: a pothole hidden in the shadows, a stray animal darting across the road, or a slower vehicle ahead. Your safe following distance needs to expand at night to accommodate the limitations of your vision.

Night driving is not just about the physical limitations imposed by darkness. It's also about acknowledging your own limitations. Fatigue creeps in faster at night, so be mindful of your energy levels. Take breaks when needed, and pull over to a safe location if you start to feel drowsy. Avoid straining your eyes by adjusting the brightness of your dashboard lights.

Alright, you now have many of the skills needed to be a safe driver. But sometimes, things go wrong. So, in the next chapter, we will look at what you can do during emergencies.

Chapter 8

Emergency Procedures

Mastering emergency procedures goes beyond simply passing the DMV written test. By understanding how to handle emergencies, you'll gain the confidence to navigate challenging situations on the road. This includes how to

- identify and react to roadside breakdowns.
- handle common emergencies like tire blowouts and engine fires.
- navigate the road safely through accidents and hazardous weather conditions.
- utilize your vehicle's safety features effectively.

A calm and collected response during an emergency can significantly improve the outcome for yourself and others on the road. So, let's buckle up and get prepared!

Handling a Flat Tire

A flat tire can be a frustrating experience, but staying calm and following the proper procedures can ensure your safety and get you back on the road quickly.

The first priority is to avoid slamming on your brakes. Panicked actions can worsen the situation. Instead, gradually apply pressure to the brake pedal to slow down steadily. As your car decelerates, turn on your hazard lights to alert other drivers of what you're going through.

Now comes the task of finding a safe place to pull over. Ideally, you want a wide shoulder with a level surface. This provides ample space to work on the tire change and minimizes the risk of the vehicle rolling. Avoid stopping on curves, hills, or narrow lanes where oncoming traffic might not see you easily.

If you're stuck on a busy road with no wide shoulder, get as far away from traffic as possible. This might involve pulling onto a median (if legal) or even a sidewalk, as long as it doesn't create further hazards for pedestrians.

Once you've found a safe spot, engage the parking brake and put your car in park (automatic) or first gear (manual). This prevents the vehicle from rolling while you work. Gather the tools you'll need for the tire change: the lug wrench, jack, and your spare tire.

Before raising the car, it's important to loosen the lug nuts on the flat tire slightly. Use the lug wrench to turn each nut one-quarter turn counter-clockwise. This will make it easier to remove them completely once the vehicle is lifted.

Your owner's manual for your car is your bible here. Consult it to locate the frame points specifically designed for using the jack. Positioning the jack on any other spot can damage your vehicle. Carefully raise the car using the jack until the flat tire is a few inches off the ground.

Now that the weight is off the flat tire, you can completely remove the loosened lug nuts and set them aside in a safe place where they won't get lost or roll away. With the nuts removed, carefully pull the flat tire straight off the hub and place it somewhere secure, like under the trunk floor (if there's space).

The spare tire should be easy to identify. Lift it and position it so the holes in the rim align perfectly with the lug bolts on the hub. Once aligned, carefully lower the spare tire onto the hub.

Here comes the crucial part of re-attaching the tire. Screw on the lug nuts by hand as tightly as possible. The goal is to get initial threading on all the nuts before tightening them further.

Once all the lug nuts are hand-tight, carefully lower the car using the jack. Now comes the most critical step, which is tightening the lug nuts in a star pattern using the wrench. Refer to your owner's manual for the recommended tightness, as overtightening can damage the threads while undertightening can cause the tire to come loose while driving.

Before getting back on the road, double-check that all the lug nuts are secure. Give each one a final tug with the wrench to ensure they haven't loosened during the process.

Finally, store the flat tire and tools securely in your vehicle. Ideally, the flat tire should be repaired or replaced by a professional as soon as possible.

If you're not certain about changing a tire, call for roadside assistance. There's no shame in seeking help, and it's always better to prioritize your safety than risk struggling with a task you're not comfortable with.

Engine Trouble

Engine trouble can range from a minor annoyance to a major concern. The key to navigating such situations is staying calm, following the proper procedures, and prioritizing your safety.

Your car often communicates its distress before things completely grind to a halt. Pay attention to the following signs:

- **Strange noises:** A knocking, grinding, or squealing coming from the engine compartment is a clear indication that something's amiss. Don't ignore these sounds, as they can point towards a developing problem.
- **Burning smells:** The unmistakable scent of burning rubber or oil is a serious warning. Pull over immediately, as it could signify overheating or a leaking component.
- **Dashboard warning lights:** Modern cars are equipped with a network of warning lights on the dashboard to indicate potential issues. Consult your owner's manual to understand the specific meaning of each symbol. Don't ignore illuminated warning lights, especially those related to the engine or temperature.
- **Reduced engine power:** If your car suddenly feels sluggish or struggles to maintain speed, it could be a sign of engine trouble. Reduced power can also be accompanied by jerking or hesitation when accelerating.
- **Vibrations:** Excessive vibrations in the steering wheel or throughout the car can indicate engine problems or issues with the drivetrain.

If you experience any of the warning signs mentioned above, the first priority is to find a safe place to pull over. Ideally, look for a wide shoulder with a level surface, away from traffic. This minimizes the risk of an accident while you assess the situation. If you're on a highway and there's no shoulder, try to make it to the nearest exit ramp before coming to a complete stop.

After pulling over to a safe location, turn on your hazard lights. This alerts other drivers to your situation and makes your vehicle more visible, which is especially important during low-light conditions or on busy roads.

Now that you're safely out of traffic, take a moment to assess the situation. Can you identify any obvious causes for the engine trouble? For example, a flat tire can cause vibrations and reduced power. However, avoid attempting major repairs on the roadside unless you're absolutely comfortable and you possess the necessary tools and expertise.

If you can't identify the problem or feel unsafe continuing, don't hesitate to call for help. Roadside assistance programs offered by your insurance company or automobile association can be lifesavers in such situations. When calling for assistance, provide them with your current location and any details you can about the problem, such as the warning lights that came on or the specific symptoms you experienced.

Skids

Skids are a frightening experience for any driver. The car suddenly feels like it's no longer responding to your steering inputs, which can throw you into a state of panic. However, by understanding the two main types of skids (understeer and oversteer) you can react more effectively and regain control of the vehicle.

Understeer Skid

You're entering a corner a little too fast. You turn the steering wheel, expecting the car to follow your lead and hug the curve. Instead, the car feels sluggish and continues moving in a relatively straight line, pushing towards the outside of the corner. This is understeer.

In an understeer skid, the front tires lose traction with the road surface. This can happen due to various reasons: entering a corner at excessive speed, braking too hard while turning, or driving on a slippery surface like rain or snow. The key characteristic of understeer is the car's unwillingness to turn despite your steering input. It feels like the front tires are simply pushing straight ahead, regardless of the direction the wheel is turned.

The most important thing to remember during an understeer skid is to **stay calm and avoid slamming on the brakes**. While the urge to brake hard might seem natural, it actually reduces grip on the front tires even further, thus worsening the situation. Instead, **ease off the accelerator pedal** gradually. As the car slows down, the front tires regain some grip, allowing you to regain steering control. Once you feel the car straighten slightly, you can gently re-initiate steering in the direction you want to go.

Oversteer Skid

Oversteer presents a different challenge. Here, the rear tires lose traction with the road, causing the back end of the car to fishtail (swinging out in one direction and then potentially snapping back in the opposite direction). This can happen due to sharp turns at high speeds, sudden maneuvers, or when you lift your foot off the accelerator pedal too quickly on a rear-wheel-drive car while cornering.

The sensation of oversteer is quite distinct. You feel like the rear end of your car is loose and wants to overtake the front, potentially throwing you into a spin.

If you find yourself in an oversteer skid, **stay calm and countersteer**. This might sound counterintuitive, but since the rear of the car is sliding outwards, you need to steer **in the direction of the skid** momentarily. For instance, if the car's rear end is swerving to the right, you'll need to quickly turn the steering wheel to the right as well. This will help correct the direction of the rear tires and bring the car back into alignment. Remember, the countersteer should be a quick corrective motion, not a sustained turn. As soon as you feel the car regaining stability, gently straighten the steering wheel and focus on maintaining control.

Practice Makes Perfect

Understanding skid dynamics is useful, but the best way to truly learn how to react effectively is through practice in a safe environment. Many driving schools offer skid control courses where you can experience controlled skids and learn the proper techniques for regaining control. This hands-on experience can significantly improve your ability to react appropriately in a real-world situation. Remember, staying calm, understanding the type of skid, and applying the appropriate corrective measures are the keys to navigating a skid safely.

Emergency Braking

Coming to a complete stop in an emergency situation requires a combination of quick thinking, proper technique, and understanding the factors that influence stopping distances.

The foundation of safe emergency braking lies in maintaining an adequate following distance, which is the space between your vehicle and the car in front of you. This buffer zone provides crucial reaction time in case of an unexpected hazard. The recommended following distance is at least **three seconds** behind the vehicle in front of you at highway speeds. However, this is a baseline, and you should adjust it based on weather conditions and traffic flow. In heavy rain, snow, or fog, where visibility is reduced, it's wise to double or even triple the following distance to allow for extra reaction time.

When faced with an emergency, your natural instinct might be to slam on the brakes as hard as possible. However, this can be counterproductive. Slamming on the brakes can lock up the wheels, causing the car to skid and potentially lose steering control. Skidding significantly increases the stopping distance and reduces your ability to maneuver around the hazard.

Apply **firm and steady pressure** on the brake pedal. This ensures maximum braking force without locking the wheels. Modern cars are often equipped with Anti-lock Braking Systems (ABS) that help prevent wheel lockup during hard braking.

If your car has ABS, you can press the brake pedal firmly and hold it down even if you feel a pulsing sensation. The ABS system is rapidly pumping the brakes for you, preventing wheel lockup and maintaining steering control. This allows you to maneuver the car around the hazard while braking to a stop.

Stopping distance is a crucial concept for safe driving. It refers to the total distance your car travels from the time you see a hazard and apply the brakes to the time you come to a complete stop. Several factors influence stopping distance, including:

- **Vehicle speed:** The faster you're going, the greater the distance required to stop.
- **Road conditions:** Wet, icy, or gravel roads significantly increase stopping distances compared to dry pavement.
- **Tire condition:** Worn or underinflated tires reduce grip and extend stopping distances.
- **Vehicle weight:** Heavier vehicles take longer to stop than lighter ones.

By maintaining a safe following distance, applying firm and steady pressure on the brakes during emergencies, and understanding the factors that influence stopping distances, you can significantly improve your safety on the road.

While emergency situations are unpredictable, you can improve your reaction time and braking skills through practice in a safe and controlled environment. Many driving schools offer courses where you can learn proper braking techniques and experience emergency braking scenarios under controlled conditions. This hands-on experience can significantly boost your confidence and ability to react effectively in a real-world emergency.

You're almost ready to take the test! In the next chapter, we will go through some test-taking tips and strategies so that, when the test day rolls around, you are at your best!

Chapter 9

Test-Taking Tips and Strategies

Congratulations! You've mastered the road rules and honed your driving skills. Now, one final hurdle stands between you and cruising down the open highway with your California driver's license: the DMV written knowledge test.

So, let's explore some effective study methods, smart answer-selection techniques, and stress-management tips to ensure you ace the written test on your first try.

Staying Calm on Test Day

The best defense against test-day jitters is thorough preparation. Instead of going for a last-minute cram, start studying early and create a study schedule that allows you to absorb information effectively. A well-rested mind is a focused mind, so prioritize a good night's sleep before the exam. Additionally, incorporating relaxation techniques like deep breathing or meditation into your routine can equip you with tools to manage stress when test day arrives.

Test anxiety often thrives on negative self-talk. Instead of letting self-doubt take hold, challenge those negative thoughts with positive affirmations. Remind yourself of your past successes and the strengths you've developed through studying. Take a moment to visualize yourself calmly and confidently taking the exam, answering each question with a clear mind. By picturing this success, you prime your mind for a positive outcome.

Even with preparation, a wave of anxiety might still hit during the exam. Deep breathing is a powerful tool in such situations. Take slow, deliberate breaths, feeling your belly rise and fall with each inhale and exhale. This simple technique can slow your heart rate and bring a sense of calm. Progressive muscle relaxation is another technique you can employ. Begin with your toes and work your way up. This can help release the physical tension that often accompanies anxiety.

If you find your mind racing, momentarily shift your focus to a calming image or memory. Visualize a peaceful scene or recall a time you felt relaxed and centered. By briefly diverting your attention, you can interrupt the anxiety cycle and regain your composure.

Acing the Test Within the Time Limit

The DMV written test comes with a time limit, and managing it effectively is crucial for success.

Familiarize yourself with the test format beforehand. Knowing the number of questions, allotted time, and any section breakdowns will help you develop a plan of attack. Consider questions with higher point values; prioritizing them allows you to earn more points within the time limit.

Once you receive the test, don't dive straight into answering questions. Take a few minutes to scan the entire test. This quick overview gives you a sense of the question types and their distribution, allowing you to budget your time effectively. Remember, some questions might require more time or thought than others.

Armed with this knowledge, allocate your time strategically. Prioritize questions with higher point values, as they contribute more significantly to your score. If you encounter a particularly challenging question, don't get bogged down. Use a marking system to flag it and move on. You can always revisit it later if time allows. Avoid spending an excessive amount of time on any single question, as this can eat into your time for the rest of the exam.

Proofreading and Avoiding Common Pitfalls

Acing the DMV written test isn't just about answering questions correctly. It's also about ensuring that your answers accurately reflect your knowledge.

Before you submit the test with a sigh of relief, dedicate some time to proofreading, if you're able. Leaving enough time at the end of the exam allows you to review your answers. This final check ensures you haven't made any careless mistakes or misinterpreted questions.

Common Pitfalls and How to Avoid Them

Test anxiety or rushing through the exam can lead to a common pitfall: misreading the question itself. Take your time to comprehend what each question is asking before jumping to conclusions. Sometimes, the answer might seem obvious at first glance, but a closer look might reveal a subtle detail that changes everything.

Pay close attention to details, especially when dealing with multiple-choice questions. A single careless mistake, like mistaking "always" for "sometimes" in an answer choice, can make a big difference. Slow down, reread the answer options, and ensure that each choice aligns with the wording of the question.

Rushing through the test is a recipe for disaster. Accuracy should take precedence over speed. Take a deep breath before answering each question and resist the urge to fly through it just to finish quickly.

Retaking the Permit Test

Even the most prepared test-taker can encounter an unexpected hurdle. If you don't pass the permit test on your first try, don't be discouraged! This setback simply means a little more preparation before you conquer the written exam.

The first step towards a successful retake is understanding why you failed in the first place. If the DMV provides feedback on your performance, utilize it to your advantage. Analyze the areas where you struggled and identify topics that require additional focus. This targeted review allows you to concentrate on your weak spots and solidify your understanding before attempting the test again.

Retaking Procedures

The process of retaking the permit test varies slightly depending on your state's regulations. It's crucial to inquire about the waiting period before you can reschedule your exam. Some states allow immediate retests, while others may require you to wait a specific period.

Gather any necessary documents and fees associated with re-registration. This might include your learner's permit, proof of identification, and the retest fee. With the administrative details ironed out, schedule your retake date at your earliest convenience.

While you wait for your retest date, don't let your studies stagnate. Utilize additional resources to solidify your understanding of the road rules and traffic laws. Consider taking practice tests online or revisiting your driver's handbook. The more you practice and refine your knowledge, the more confident you'll feel approaching the retest.

Now, it's time to give a rundown of the actual test. The next chapter will be a mock exam that uses real questions from the test to help you master it!

Chapter 10

Mock Permit Test Questions and Explanations

The purpose of this mock exam is to both get you comfortable with the final test and to ensure you have all the knowledge you need to pass. Start by taking the test and marking yourself using a separate sheet of paper. Then, focus on restudying only the questions you got wrong. Once you feel confident, retake the test. Rinse and repeat until you get every answer correct. By doing so, you will guarantee that you can pass the DMV the first time!

Final Tips Before You Take the Mock Test

The California DMV written test loves to throw similar-sounding answers at you. Don't get flustered! Treat the question like a detective story. Read it thoroughly, paying close attention to keywords and the specific situation it describes. Is it about understanding right-of-way at an intersection, following distance on the highway, or handling a disabled vehicle? Understanding the scenario is crucial.

Sometimes, there are choices that blatantly contradict safe driving practices or traffic laws. These are the easy ones! Eliminate them right away. For example, if the question asks about following distance and an answer says "Stay bumper-to-bumper," you can confidently cross that one off.

What's the core concept that the question is really testing? Is it about maintaining a safe following distance or using your brakes properly? Pinpointing the key concept helps you focus on the relevant answer choices.

Now that you've narrowed it down, compare the remaining answers. Choose the one that best aligns with the key concept and promotes safe driving practices. Think defensive driving—what would a responsible driver do in this situation?

Still stuck between two seemingly good answers? Don't panic! Use process of elimination. Based on your knowledge of traffic laws, eliminate the answer that sounds less likely to be the safest or most appropriate course of action.

The more practice tests you take, the more you'll see patterns in how answer choices are presented and explained. This will sharpen your skills in identifying the best answer, even when the options look like close cousins.

Okay, then. Are you ready to take the mock exam?

Mock Exam

Circle the answer you believe is correct, or write it down on a separate page.

Q1: What does a stop sign mean?

    A.   Slow down and proceed with caution.

    B.   Stop only if there is traffic.

    C.   Stop completely and proceed when safe.

    D.   Yield to oncoming traffic.

Q2: What should you do when you see a yield sign?

A. Bring your vehicle to a complete stop right away.

B. Slow down and be prepared to stop if necessary.

C. Speed up so that you can catch up with other cars.

D. Disregard if there are no other cars around.

Q3: What does a speed limit sign indicate?

A. The minimum speed you should travel

B. The maximum speed you are allowed to travel under ideal conditions

C. The exact speed you must travel

D. A suggested speed for the area

Q4: What does a "Slippery When Wet" sign mean?

A. The road is always slippery.

B. The road is slippery when it is raining or wet.

C. The road has sharp turns ahead.

D. The road is closed when wet.

Q5: What should you do when you see a "Curve Ahead" sign?

A. Maintain your current speed.

B. Slow down and be prepared for a change in direction.

C. Stop immediately.

D. Speed up to navigate the curve.

Q6: What is the purpose of a "School Zone" sign?

    A.   To indicate a nearby school playground

    B.   To warn drivers to be cautious and watch for children

    C.   To inform drivers of a school bus stop ahead

    D.   To indicate a pedestrian crossing

Q7: What does a route marker sign indicate?

    A.   The speed limit on a particular road

    B.   The direction and distance to a specific destination

    C.   The name of the road you are currently on

    D.   The road's history and significance

Q8: What should you do when you see an exit sign on the freeway?

    A.   Prepare to exit if that is your intended destination.

    B.   Ignore it unless you are lost.

    C.   Speed up to pass other vehicles.

    D.   Stop immediately if you need to exit.

Q9: What is the purpose of a "Hospital" sign?

    A.   To indicate a nearby emergency medical facility

    B.   To warn of traffic congestion

    C.   To inform drivers of a hospital bus stop

    D.   To indicate a pedestrian crossing

Q10: What does a red traffic light mean?

A. Proceed with caution.

B. Stop and wait until the light turns green.

C. Slow down and yield.

D. Speed up to pass through the intersection.

Q11: What should you do when you see a yellow traffic light?

A. Speed up to get through the intersection quickly.

B. Slow down and prepare to stop if it is safe to do so.

C. Ignore it and continue at your current speed.

D. Stop immediately.

Q12: What does a green traffic light mean?

A. Slow down.

B. Proceed if the intersection is clear.

C. Come to a full stop.

D. Yield to oncoming traffic.

Q13: Who has the right of way at a four-way stop?

A. The driver who reaches the intersection first

B. The driver going straight

C. The driver on the left

D. The driver on the right

Q14: When merging onto the freeway, who has the right of way?

A. The vehicle merging onto the freeway

B. The vehicles already on the freeway

C. The larger vehicle

D. The fastest vehicle

Q15: When must a driver yield to pedestrians?

A. Only at marked crosswalks

B. Only at intersections with traffic signals

C. At all crosswalks, marked or unmarked

D. Only when pedestrians are in the same lane

Q16: What is the maximum speed limit on most California highways?

A. 50 mph

B. 65 mph

C. 75 mph

D. 80 mph

Q17: What should you do when driving conditions are poor?

A. Pull over and wait for conditions to improve.

B. Increase your following distance and reduce your speed.

C. Flash your hazards and honk your horn.

D. Drive normally.

Q18: When driving in a residential area, what is the typical speed limit?

    A. 10 mph

    B. 15 mph

    C. 25 mph

    D. 35 mph

Q19: What should you do before changing lanes?

    A. Speed up to match the speed of the cars in the next lane.

    B. Signal, check mirrors, and look over your shoulder.

    C. Change lanes quickly without signaling.

    D. Slow down and change lanes carefully.

Q20: Which lane should you use if you are driving slower than the flow of traffic on a multi-lane highway?

    A. The right lane

    B. The center lane

    C. Any lane

    D. The left lane

Q21: When is it legal to drive in a bicycle lane?

    A. Always, if no bicycles are present

    B. Only when preparing for a turn within 200 feet

    C. When driving a motorcycle

    D. When avoiding an obstacle

Q22: What is the first step you should take when preparing to pass another vehicle?

A. Signal your intention to pass.

B. Increase your speed.

C. Move into the left lane.

D. Flash your headlights.

Q23: When is it illegal to pass another vehicle?

A. On a two-way street

B. On a multi-lane highway

C. Within 100 feet of an intersection or railroad crossing

D. When driving during the day

Q24: What should you do after passing another vehicle?

A. Return to your lane immediately.

B. Wait until you see the vehicle you passed in your rearview mirror before returning to your lane.

C. Stay in the left lane.

D. Slow down.

Q25: What does a red curb mean?

A. You may park for a limited time

B. Loading and unloading zone only

C. No stopping, standing, or parking

D. Parking for disabled persons only

Q26: How far must you park from a fire hydrant?

   A.   At least 5 feet

   B.   At least 15 feet

   C.   At least 25 feet

   D.   At least 35 feet

Q27: When is it illegal to park on a freeway?

   A.   Only during rush hour

   B.   Always, unless there is an emergency

   C.   If you are stopping for a rest

   D.   If you have a flat tire

Q28: What should you do to maintain control of your vehicle while steering?

   A.   Place one hand on the wheel.

   B.   Place both hands on the wheel, with hands at the 9 and 3 o'clock positions.

   C.   Place both hands on the wheel, with hands at the 10 and 2 o'clock positions.

   D.   Place only your fingertips on the wheel.

Q29: How should you apply the brakes to make a smooth stop?

   A.   Step on the brakes with force.

   B.   Apply steady pressure to the brake pedal.

   C.   Pump the brakes every five seconds.

    D.   Release the accelerator and wait for the car to stop.

Q30: What is the correct way to accelerate your vehicle?

    A.   Press the accelerator quickly.

    B.   Gradually press down on the accelerator.

    C.   Keep your foot on the brake while accelerating.

    D.   Accelerate only in short bursts.

Q31: What should you check before starting your vehicle?

    A.   Only the fuel level

    B.   Lights, tires, and fluids

    C.   Only the tire pressure

    D.   Only the oil level

Q32: How often should you check your vehicle's tire pressure?

    A.   Once a month

    B.   Every three months

    C.   Twice a year

    D.   Only before long trips

Q33: What should you do if you notice that one of your vehicle's lights is not working?

    A.   Ignore it and continue driving.

    B.   Replace the light as soon as possible.

    C.   Drive only during the day.

    D.   Use your hazard lights instead.

Q34: What is the recommended following distance under normal driving conditions?

    A.   One second

    B.   Two seconds

    C.   Three seconds

    D.   Four seconds

Q35: How should you adjust your following distance in bad weather?

    A.   Decrease your following distance.

    B.   Keep the same following distance.

    C.   Increase your following distance.

    D.   Ignore following distance.

Q36: What is the main reason for maintaining a safe following distance?

    A.   To save fuel

    B.   To have enough time to react to sudden stops

    C.   To prevent other drivers from passing

    D.   To avoid speeding

Q37: How should you pass a bicycle on the road?

    A.   Pass closely to give more room to oncoming traffic.

    B.   Pass with at least three feet of clearance.

    C.   Honk your horn to alert the cyclist.

D. Pass as quickly as possible.

Q38: What is the best way to drive safely around large trucks?

A. Drive in the truck's blind spots.

B. Pass quickly on the right side.

C. Maintain a safe following distance and pass on the left side.

D. Drive closely behind the truck to draft.

Q39: What should you do when you see a motorcycle ahead of you?

A. Make sure to catch up with the motorcycle.

B. Maintain a safe following distance.

C. Drive very close to the motorcycle.

D. Honk your horn to alert the motorcyclist.

Q40: What is a good habit to avoid distractions while driving?

A. Use your phone only at stoplights.

B. Keep your phone in a location where you can easily reach it.

C. Use hands-free devices and avoid multitasking.

D. Check your phone only if it rings.

Q41: What should you do when driving at night to ensure safety?

A. Use your high beams at all times.

B. Reduce your speed and use your low beams.

C. Follow closely behind other vehicles to see better.

D. Only drive on well-lit roads.

Q42: What is the best way to avoid fatigue while driving?

A. Drink caffeinated beverages continuously.

B. Drive with the windows down.

C. Take regular interludes and get plenty of rest before driving.

D. Play loud music to stay awake.

Q43: When making a left turn at an intersection, you should:

A. Yield to oncoming traffic and pedestrians.

B. Turn immediately when the light turns green.

C. Only yield to vehicles on your right.

D. Not signal your turn.

Q44: In which situation is it legal to make a U-turn?

A. On a street where cars drive in just one direction

B. When you encounter a "No U-turn" sign on an intersection

C. Across a double yellow line when it is safe and legal

D. In front of a fire station

Q45: What should you do before making a U-turn?

A. Check for traffic and pedestrians and signal your intention.

B. Speed up and turn quickly.

C. Honk your horn to alert other drivers.

D. Make the turn without signaling.

Q46: When approaching a roundabout, you should:

A. Enter the roundabout at full speed.

B. Yield to traffic already in the roundabout.

C. Stop in the roundabout if you miss your exit.

D. Signal left when entering the roundabout.

Q47: What is the correct way to navigate a roundabout?

A. Enter and drive clockwise.

B. Enter and drive counterclockwise.

C. Enter without yielding.

D. Change lanes frequently within the roundabout.

Q48: How should you handle an interchange?

A. Merge smoothly into traffic and follow signs to your destination.

B. Stop at the merge point to check for traffic.

C. Ignore lane markings and proceed as you wish.

D. Exit the interchange at the first opportunity.

Q49: What should you do when driving in a school zone?

A. Ignore the posted speed limit.

B. Reduce your speed and watch for children.

C. Speed up to clear the area quickly.

D.   Only follow the speed limit during school hours.

Q50: How should you drive in a construction zone?

    A.   Maintain your normal speed.

    B.   Increase your speed to avoid delays.

    C.   Slow down and follow posted signs and instructions.

    D.   Ignore construction workers and proceed as usual.

Q51: When are you required to follow the speed limit in a school zone?

    A.   Only during school hours

    B.   When children are present

    C.   Only on school days

    D.   At all times, regardless of the presence of children

Q52: What should you do when driving in the rain?

    A.   Drive as you normally would.

    B.   Use your high beams.

    C.   Slow down and increase your following distance.

    D.   Speed up to avoid getting wet.

Q53: How should you drive in foggy conditions?

    A.   Use your high beams.

    B.   Use your low beams and drive at a reduced speed.

    C.   Turn off your headlights.

    D.   Drive at normal speed.

Q54: What should you do when driving in snow or ice?

    A.   Use your cruise control.

    B.   Accelerate and decelerate quickly.

    C.   Slow down, increase following distance, and brake gently.

    D.   Drive as you normally would.

Q55: What should you do if you experience a tire blowout?

    A.   Slam on the brakes.

    B.   Hold the steering wheel firmly, gradually slow down, and pull off the road.

    C.   Immediately swerve to the side of the road.

    D.   Speed up to get off the road quickly.

Q56: What should you do if your engine fails while driving?

    A.   Continue driving until you reach a service station.

    B.   Turn off the ignition immediately.

    C.   Shift to neutral, try to restart the engine, and safely pull off the road.

    D.   Abandon the vehicle in the lane.

Q57: What should you do if your brakes fail while driving?

    A.   Shift to a lower gear and pump the brake pedal.

    B.   Turn off the engine.

    C.   Speed up to clear the area.

    D.   Jump out of the vehicle.

Answers With Explanations

Q1: What does a stop sign mean?

Correct Answer: Stop completely and proceed when safe

Explanation: A stop sign requires drivers to come to a complete stop at the limit line, crosswalk, or before entering the intersection. This ensures that drivers have the opportunity to observe any oncoming traffic or pedestrians and proceed only when it is safe to do so. This practice minimizes the risk of collisions and promotes road safety.

Q2: What should you do when you see a yield sign?

Correct Answer: Slow down and be prepared to stop if necessary

Explanation: A yield sign indicates that drivers must slow down and be prepared to stop if necessary to give right-of-way to other vehicles or pedestrians. Yielding helps prevent accidents by ensuring that drivers do not enter a road or intersection without considering the traffic already there, thus ensuring a smoother and safer flow of traffic.

Q3: What does a speed limit sign indicate?

Correct Answer: The maximum speed you are allowed to travel under ideal conditions

Explanation: A speed limit sign indicates the maximum speed that vehicles are legally allowed to travel on a particular stretch of road under ideal conditions. It is important for safety as it helps to regulate traffic speed, reducing the risk of accidents due to speeding or traveling at unsafe speeds for the given road conditions.

Q4: What does a "Slippery When Wet" sign mean?

Correct Answer: The road is slippery when it is raining or wet

Explanation: This sign warns drivers that the road may become slippery when wet, such as during or after rain. Drivers should reduce their speed and drive cautiously to maintain control of their vehicle, as wet conditions can reduce traction and increase stopping distances.

Q5: What should you do when you see a "Curve Ahead" sign?

Correct Answer: Slow down and be prepared for a change in direction

Explanation: A "Curve Ahead" sign indicates that there is a curve in the road ahead. Drivers should slow down to a safe speed that allows them to navigate the curve safely, as higher speeds can increase the risk of losing control of the vehicle.

Q6: What is the purpose of a "School Zone" sign?

Correct Answer: To warn drivers to be cautious and watch for children

Explanation: A "School Zone" sign alerts drivers that they are entering an area near a school where children may be present. Drivers should reduce their speed, be extra vigilant, and be prepared to stop for children crossing the road or for school buses that are loading or unloading children.

Q7: What does a route marker sign indicate?

Correct Answer: The direction and distance to a specific destination

Explanation: Route marker signs provide information about the direction and distance to specific destinations, such as towns, cities, or highways. These signs help drivers navigate and reach their intended destinations efficiently and safely.

Q8: What should you do when you see an exit sign on the freeway?

Correct Answer: Prepare to exit if that is your intended destination

Explanation: An exit sign indicates an upcoming exit from the freeway. Drivers who intend to take the exit should prepare to do so by safely changing lanes if necessary and reducing speed in preparation for leaving the freeway. Ignoring the sign could result in missing the intended exit or having to perform unsafe last-minute maneuvers.

Q9: What is the purpose of a "Hospital" sign?

Correct Answer: To indicate a nearby emergency medical facility

Explanation: A "Hospital" sign directs drivers to a nearby emergency medical facility. This information is crucial in emergencies when quick access to medical care is needed. It ensures that drivers can locate the hospital quickly and efficiently.

Q10: What does a red traffic light mean?

Correct Answer: Stop and wait until the light turns green

Explanation: A red traffic light requires drivers to come to a complete stop and wait until the light turns green before proceeding. This rule is fundamental to traffic control, preventing collisions at intersections by clearly indicating when it is safe to go and when to stop.

Q11: What should you do when you see a yellow traffic light?

Correct Answer: Slow down and prepare to stop if it is safe to do so

Explanation: A yellow traffic light signals that the light is about to turn red. Drivers should slow down and prepare to stop if it is safe to do so. Rushing through a yellow light can be dangerous, as the light may change to red while the driver is still in the intersection, increasing the risk of collisions.

Q12: What does a green traffic light mean?

Correct Answer: Proceed if the intersection is clear

Explanation: A green traffic light means that drivers may proceed through the intersection, but only if it is clear of other vehicles and pedestrians. It is important to still check the intersection for any potential hazards before proceeding, as some drivers or pedestrians may not follow traffic signals correctly.

Q13: Who has the right of way at a four-way stop?

Correct Answer: The driver who reaches the intersection first

Explanation: At a four-way stop, the driver who arrives first has the right of way. This rule helps to ensure an orderly flow of traffic and reduces confusion about who should proceed first, thus minimizing the risk of accidents.

Q14: When merging onto the freeway, who has the right of way?

Correct Answer: The vehicles already on the freeway

Explanation: Vehicles already traveling on the freeway have the right of way. Drivers merging onto the freeway must adjust their speed and merge safely without disrupting the flow of traffic. This rule helps maintain a consistent and safe speed on the freeway, reducing the risk of collisions.

Q15: When must a driver yield to pedestrians?

Correct Answer: At all crosswalks, marked or unmarked

Explanation: Drivers must yield to pedestrians at all crosswalks, whether they are marked or unmarked. This ensures the safety of pedestrians, giving them the right of way when crossing the street and reducing the risk of pedestrian-related accidents.

Q16: What is the maximum speed limit on most California highways?

Correct Answer: 65 mph

Explanation: The maximum speed limit on most California highways is 65 mph. This speed limit helps to regulate traffic flow and maintain safety on highways, ensuring that vehicles travel at a speed that is manageable and reduces the likelihood of high-speed collisions.

Q17: What should you do when driving conditions are poor?

Correct Answer: Increase your following distance, and reduce your speed

Explanation: A three-second following distance is recommended under normal driving conditions. However, if driving conditions are poor, you should increase your following distance to give you more time to react.

Q18: When driving in a residential area, what is the typical speed limit?

Correct Answer: 25 mph

Explanation: The typical speed limit in residential areas is 25 mph. This lower speed limit is important for the safety of residents, including children playing, pedestrians, and pets, as it gives drivers more time to react to any unexpected events.

Q19: What should you do before changing lanes?

Correct Answer: Signal, check mirrors, and look over your shoulder

Explanation: Before changing lanes, drivers should signal their intention, check their mirrors, and look over their shoulder to check their blind spots. This ensures that the lane change is made safely, without cutting off or colliding with other vehicles.

Q20: Which lane should you use if you are driving slower than the flow of traffic on a multi-lane highway?

Correct Answer: The right lane

Explanation: Drivers traveling slower than the flow of traffic should use the right lane. This allows faster-moving traffic to pass safely on the left and helps to maintain a steady flow of traffic, reducing the risk of congestion and accidents.

Q21: When is it legal to drive in a bicycle lane?

Correct Answer: Only when preparing for a turn within 200 feet

Explanation: It is legal to drive in a bicycle lane only when preparing for a turn within 200 feet. This rule helps to ensure the safety of bicyclists by minimizing the amount of time that vehicles spend in the bicycle lane and reducing the potential for conflicts.

Q22: What is the first step you should take when preparing to pass another vehicle?

Correct Answer: Signal your intention to pass

Explanation: The first step when preparing to pass another vehicle is to signal your intention. This communicates your planned maneuver to other drivers, allowing them to adjust accordingly and helping to prevent accidents caused by sudden, unexpected lane changes.

Q23: When is it illegal to pass another vehicle?

Correct Answer: Within 100 feet of an intersection or railroad crossing

Explanation: It is illegal to pass another vehicle within 100 feet of an intersection or railroad crossing because these areas require extra caution. Passing in these areas can increase the risk of collisions with vehicles entering the intersection or crossing the tracks.

Q24: What should you do after passing another vehicle?

Correct Answer: Wait until you see the vehicle you passed in your rearview mirror before returning to your lane

Explanation: After passing another vehicle, you should wait until you can see the vehicle in your rearview mirror before returning to your lane. This ensures that you have enough distance to return safely without cutting off the other vehicle.

Q25: What does a red curb mean?

Correct Answer: No stopping, standing, or parking

Explanation: A red curb indicates that stopping, standing, or parking is not allowed. This rule helps to ensure that certain areas remain clear for emergency vehicles or other essential uses, promoting safety and accessibility.

Q26: How far must you park from a fire hydrant?

Correct Answer: At least 15 feet

Explanation: You must park at least 15 feet from a fire hydrant. This distance ensures that fire trucks have adequate access to the hydrant in case of a fire, enabling firefighters to quickly connect hoses and access water.

Q27: When is it illegal to park on a freeway?

Correct Answer: Always, unless there is an emergency

Explanation: It is illegal to park on a freeway unless there is an emergency. Freeways are designed for high-speed travel, and parked vehicles can create dangerous obstacles, increasing the risk of accidents. In case of an emergency, drivers should use emergency flashers and move their vehicles as far off the road as possible.

Q28: What should you do to maintain control of your vehicle while steering?

Correct Answer: Use both hands on the wheel, with hands at the 9 and 3 o'clock positions

Explanation: Using both hands on the wheel at the 9 and 3 o'clock positions provides better control and balance while steering. This position helps in making smoother turns and allows for quick reactions in case of emergencies, which improves overall driving safety.

Q29: How should you apply the brakes to make a smooth stop?

Correct Answer: Apply steady pressure to the brake pedal

Explanation: Applying steady pressure to the brake pedal allows for a gradual and smooth stop, reducing the risk of skidding or losing control. This method helps to maintain control of the vehicle and provides a comfortable experience for passengers.

Q30: What is the correct way to accelerate your vehicle?

Correct Answer: Gradually press down on the accelerator

Explanation: Gradually pressing down on the accelerator ensures smooth and controlled acceleration, which helps to prevent wheel spin and loss of traction. This method also promotes better fuel efficiency and reduces wear and tear on the vehicle.

Q31: What should you check before starting your vehicle?

Correct Answer: Lights, tires, and fluids

Explanation: Checking the lights, tires, and fluids before starting your vehicle ensures that all essential components are functioning properly. This pre-drive check helps to prevent breakdowns and ensures that the vehicle is safe to operate.

Q32: How often should you check your vehicle's tire pressure?

Correct Answer: Once a month

Explanation: Checking tire pressure once a month helps to maintain optimal tire performance, fuel efficiency, and safety. Properly inflated tires reduce the risk of blowouts and improve the vehicle's handling.

Q33: What should you do if you notice that one of your vehicle's lights is not working?

Correct Answer: Replace the light as soon as possible

Explanation: Replacing a non-working light as soon as possible is crucial for safe driving. Functional lights are essential for visibility and communication with other drivers, especially in low-light conditions or at night.

Q34: What is the recommended following distance under normal driving conditions?

Correct Answer: Three seconds

Explanation: A three-second following distance under normal driving conditions provides enough time to react and stop safely if the vehicle ahead suddenly brakes. This distance helps to prevent rear-end collisions and ensures a safe driving environment.

Q35: How should you adjust your following distance in bad weather?

Correct Answer: Increase your following distance

Explanation: Increasing your following distance in bad weather allows for more reaction time and reduces the risk of collisions. Adverse weather conditions can affect visibility and stopping distances, so maintaining a greater distance helps to ensure safety.

Q36: What is the main reason for maintaining a safe following distance?

Correct Answer: To have enough time to react to sudden stops

Explanation: The main reason for maintaining a safe following distance is to provide enough time to react to sudden stops or emergencies. This practice helps to avoid rear-ending.

Q37: How should you pass a bicycle on the road?

Correct Answer: Pass with at least three feet of clearance

Explanation: Passing with at least three feet of clearance provides a safe distance between the vehicle and the cyclist, reducing the risk of collisions and ensuring the cyclist's safety. This buffer allows for unexpected movements by the cyclist and helps to prevent accidents.

Q38: What is the best way to drive safely around large trucks?

Correct Answer: Maintain a safe following distance and pass on the left side

Explanation: Maintaining a safe following distance and passing on the left side of large trucks ensures that you are visible to the truck driver and reduces the risk of being in the truck's blind spots. Passing on the left is typically safer because the driver's visibility is better on that side.

Q39: What should you do when you see a motorcycle ahead of you?

Correct Answer: Maintain a safe following distance

Explanation: Maintaining a safe following distance when you see a motorcycle ahead ensures that you have enough time to react to the motorcycle's movements. Motorcycles can stop more quickly and maneuver differently than cars, so a greater distance helps to prevent accidents.

Q40: What is a good habit to avoid distractions while driving?

Correct Answer: Use hands-free devices and avoid multitasking

Explanation: Using hands-free devices and avoiding multitasking minimizes distractions and keeps your focus on driving. This practice reduces the risk of accidents caused by distracted driving and helps to maintain control of the vehicle.

Q41: What should you do when driving at night to ensure safety?

Correct Answer: Reduce your speed and use your low beams

Explanation: Reducing your speed and using your low beams at night enhances visibility and reduces glare for oncoming drivers. Driving slower allows more time to react to hazards that are harder to see in the dark, thus improving overall safety.

Q42: What is the best way to avoid fatigue while driving?

Correct Answer: Take regular breaks and get plenty of rest before driving

Explanation: Taking regular breaks and getting plenty of rest before driving helps to prevent fatigue. Fatigue can impair reaction time, decision-making, and overall driving performance, so staying well-rested is crucial for safe driving.

Q43: When making a left turn at an intersection, you should:

Correct Answer: Yield to oncoming traffic and pedestrians

Explanation: When making a left turn, you must yield to oncoming traffic and pedestrians crossing the intersection. This ensures that you do not collide with other vehicles or pedestrians, following safe driving practices and traffic laws.

Q44: In which situation is it legal to make a U-turn?

Correct Answer: Across a double yellow line when it is safe and legal

Explanation: Making a U-turn across a double yellow line is legal when it is safe to do so and there are no signs prohibiting U-turns. This maneuver should be done with caution and in compliance with traffic regulations.

Q45: What should you do before making a U-turn?

Correct Answer: Check for traffic and pedestrians and signal your intention

Explanation: Before making a U-turn, you should always check for traffic and pedestrians to ensure it is safe. Signaling your intention informs other drivers of your planned action, reducing the risk of accidents and promoting road safety.

Q46: When approaching a roundabout, you should:

Correct Answer: Yield to traffic already in the roundabout

Explanation: Yielding to traffic already in the roundabout prevents collisions and ensures a smooth flow of vehicles. This practice aligns with roundabout rules and promotes safe navigation through the intersection.

Q47: What is the correct way to navigate a roundabout?

Correct Answer: Enter and drive counterclockwise

Explanation: In the United States, roundabouts are navigated counterclockwise. Entering and driving counterclockwise ensures that you follow the intended traffic flow, reducing the risk of accidents and confusion.

Q48: How should you handle an interchange?

Correct Answer: Merge smoothly into traffic and follow signs to your destination

Explanation: Merging smoothly into traffic and following signs helps you navigate interchanges safely and efficiently. This practice reduces the risk of collisions and ensures that you reach your destination without confusion.

Q49: What should you do when driving in a school zone?

Correct Answer: Reduce your speed and watch for children

Explanation: Reducing your speed and watching for children in a school zone enhances safety. Children may suddenly cross the road, and driving at a lower speed gives you more time to react and prevent accidents.

Q50: How should you drive in a construction zone?

Correct Answer: Slow down and follow posted signs and instructions

Explanation: Slowing down and following posted signs in a construction zone helps to protect construction workers and other drivers. Adhering to these instructions ensures safe navigation through the construction area.

Q51: When are you required to follow the speed limit in a school zone?

Correct Answer: When children are present

Explanation: The speed limit in a school zone must be followed when children are present, ensuring their safety as they may be crossing the road or playing nearby. This practice helps to prevent accidents and protect young pedestrians.

Q52: What should you do when driving in the rain?

Correct Answer: Slow down and increase your following distance

Explanation: Slowing down and increasing your following distance in rain improves safety by providing more time to react to other vehicles and road conditions. Wet roads reduce traction, so extra caution is necessary to prevent skidding and collisions.

Q53: How should you drive in foggy conditions?

Correct Answer: Use your low beams and drive at a reduced speed

Explanation: Using low beams and driving at a reduced speed in foggy conditions improves visibility and reduces glare. High beams can reflect off the fog, making it harder to see, while low beams help you see the road and other vehicles more clearly.

Q54: What should you do when driving in snow or ice?

Correct Answer: Slow down, increase following distance, and brake gently

Explanation: Slowing down, increasing your following distance, and braking gently in snow or ice reduces the risk of losing control. These conditions require careful driving to maintain traction and avoid skidding.

Q55: What should you do if you experience a tire blowout?

Correct Answer: Hold the steering wheel firmly, gradually slow down, and pull off the road

Explanation: Holding the steering wheel firmly, gradually slowing down, and pulling off the road helps you maintain control of the vehicle during a tire blowout. This approach minimizes the risk of an accident and allows you to safely address the situation.

Q56: What should you do if your engine fails while driving?

Correct Answer: Shift to neutral, try to restart the engine, and safely pull off the road

Explanation: Shifting to neutral, attempting to restart the engine, and safely pulling off the road can ensure that you handle the engine failure without causing a traffic hazard. This practice helps you manage the situation calmly and safely.

Q57: What should you do if your brakes fail while driving?

Correct Answer: Shift to a lower gear and pump the brake pedal

Explanation: Shifting to a lower gear and pumping the brake pedal can help to regain braking power and slow the vehicle down. This approach gives you a better chance of safely stopping the vehicle and avoiding an accident.

Conclusion

You are now equipped with the knowledge you need to navigate the roads with confidence. You've grasped key concepts like traffic laws, road signs, and safe driving maneuvers. You also learned how to share the road with others.

But knowledge is only the first step. Now, you need to translate it into responsible habits. Always prioritize safety behind the wheel. Buckle up every time, stay alert, and avoid distractions. Remember, the road is a shared space, and courtesy goes a long way in preventing accidents.

We hope this book has proven to be a valuable resource in your driving education. If you found this book helpful, please consider leaving a review to help others on their path to becoming safe California drivers.

We wish you the very best of luck on your permit test and your exciting journey as a new driver!

Glossary

AB 60 License: A type of driver's license issued to undocumented immigrants in California, allowing them to drive legally in the state.

Accident report: A detailed account of an accident involving one or more vehicles, including the circumstances, involved parties, and damages; often required for insurance and legal purposes.

Bike lane: A designated lane on a roadway for the exclusive use of bicycles, marked with painted lines or symbols.

Blind intersection: An intersection where visibility is obstructed due to buildings, trees, or other structures, making it difficult for drivers to see cross traffic.

Blind spot: The areas around a vehicle that cannot be directly observed by the driver while looking forward or through the rearview mirrors.

California Driver Handbook: The official guide published by the California Department of Motor Vehicles (DMV) that contains all the rules and regulations for driving in California.

Carpool lane: A designated lane on certain highways reserved for vehicles with multiple passengers (high-occupancy vehicles) to encourage carpooling and reduce traffic congestion.

Checkpoint: A location where law enforcement officers stop vehicles to check for compliance with traffic laws, such as sobriety or license checks.

Defensive driving: A driving technique that involves being aware of potential hazards, anticipating other drivers' actions, and taking proactive steps to avoid accidents.

DMV (Department of Motor Vehicles): The state agency responsible for issuing driver's licenses, facilitating vehicle registrations, and maintaining driving records in California.

Driving Under the Influence (DUI): Operating a vehicle while impaired by alcohol or drugs; an act that is illegal and punishable by fines, license suspension, and other penalties.

GDL (Graduated Driver Licensing): A system that introduces driving privileges in stages for new drivers, typically including a learner's permit, provisional license, and full license.

Hazard lights: Flashing lights on a vehicle used to alert other drivers to a temporary hazard or emergency situation.

Intersection control: The management of traffic flow at an intersection, typically using traffic signals, stop signs, or yield signs.

Junction: A point where two or more roads meet or cross; can include intersections or merges.

LC (Learner's Permit): A restricted license that allows a new driver to practice driving under the supervision of a licensed adult.

MV (Motor vehicle): Any self-propelled vehicle used for transportation, including cars, trucks, motorcycles, and buses.

No-Zone: The areas around large trucks where the driver's visibility is limited, including the front, sides, and rear of the truck.

Parallel parking: A parking maneuver where a vehicle is parked parallel to the curb between two other parked vehicles.

Provisional license: A type of driver's license for new drivers under the age of 18; comes with certain restrictions until the driver reaches a certain age or driving experience level.

Reinstatement: The process of restoring a driver's license after it has been suspended or revoked.

Road test: A driving examination that assesses a driver's ability to operate a vehicle safely and in accordance with traffic laws.

Roadway: The portion of a street or highway used for vehicular travel, including lanes, shoulders, and any other paved surfaces.

Safety belt: A harness designed to keep occupants of a vehicle securely in place during a crash or sudden stop; commonly referred to as a seatbelt.

Traffic citation: A formal notice issued to a driver for violating traffic laws; may result in fines or points on the driver's record.

Traffic flow: The movement of vehicles and pedestrians on roadways and intersections, influenced by signals, signs, and road conditions.

Vehicle registration: The process of officially recording a vehicle with the DMV; includes obtaining a license plate and registration sticker.

Vision test: An examination to assess a driver's ability to see clearly and meet the minimum vision requirements for driving.

Yield: To allow other vehicles or pedestrians to proceed before you, as signified by a yield sign at intersections.

References

akhila. (2019, January 31). *Driving in California | Road rules & driving tips from SIXT.* SIXT Rent a Car Magazine. https://www.sixt.com/magazine/tips/driving-tips-california/

Behind-the-wheel drive test preparation. (n.d.). California DMV. Retrieved July 8, 2024, from https://www.dmv.ca.gov/portal/driver-education-and-safety/educational-materials/fast-facts/preparing-for-your-driving-test-ffdl-22/

Bicyclist and pedestrian safety. (n.d.). California DMV. Retrieved July 10, 2024, from https://www.dmv.ca.gov/portal/driver-education-and-safety/special-interest-driver-guides/bicyclists-pedestrians/

California road signs and their meanings. (2024, March 5). Best Online Traffic School. https://www.bestonlinetrafficschool.co/california-road-signs/

California state road signs/Traffic signs photos and meanings. (n.d.). driverseducationusa.com. Retrieved July 12, 2024, from https://www.driverseducationusa.com/resources/traffic-signs/

California State Transportation Agency. (2014). *California Manual on Uniform Traffic Control Devices.* https://dot.ca.gov/-/media/dot-media/programs/safety-programs/documents/signs/ca-sign-chart-2014-rev3-a11y.pdf

Driving in California. (2014, October 23). Visit California. https://www.visitcalifornia.com/experience/driving-california

Laws and rules of the road. (n.d.). California DMV. Retrieved July 13, 2024, from https://www.dmv.ca.gov/portal/handbook/california-driver-handbook/laws-and-rules-of-the-road/

Pre-drive checklist (Safety criteria). (n.d.). California DMV. Retrieved July 13, 2024, from https://www.dmv.ca.gov/portal/handbook/driving-test-criteria/pre-drive-checklist-safety-criteria/

Sample Class C Drivers Written Test 1. (n.d.). California DMV. Retrieved July 22, 2024, from https://www.dmv.ca.gov/portal/driver-education-and-safety/educational-materials/sample-driver-license-dl-knowledge-tests/sample-class-c-drivers-written-test-1/

Share the Road. (n.d.). Go Safely CA. Retrieved July 14, 2024, from https://gosafelyca.org/share-the-road/

Image Credits

Images of road signs in Chapter 4 were sourced from the *California Manual on Uniform Traffic Control Devices, Revision 3* (2014).

Made in the USA
Las Vegas, NV
16 November 2024

11950684R00085